THE TIMELINE

of

JAMAICA

I0152691

The Birth and Shaping of a Nation
Pre-1494 - 1962

GLEN CARTY

FIWIROOTS
PUBLISHING

An earlier version of this timeline was published online as part of a larger project by FiwiRoots Publishing. This edition has been revised, edited, and expanded for print publication.

INTRODUCTION

Most historical works on Jamaica's history focus on specific eras —such as slavery, the colonial period, or independence. Few attempt to cover its full historical arc in a structured timeline. This book seeks to do just that.

From first contact to full independence, The Timeline of Jamaica offers a comprehensive exploration of the key years that shaped the island's identity. Beginning with the Taíno people and the arrival of Columbus in 1494, the story unfolds through centuries of colonization, slavery, rebellion, and resistance. With a focus on pivotal years, this work traces Jamaica's transformation from a neglected Spanish outpost into a powerhouse of British colonial wealth—and ultimately into a proud, independent nation.

Carefully structured and richly detailed, the timeline captures the forces that defined Jamaica's past: the brutality of the plantation system, the long struggle for emancipation, the rise of a multicultural society forged through displacement and migration, and the island's evolving quest for self-governance. It also examines Jamaica's role in major global events—from wars to shifting trade networks—and how these moments helped shape the island's economy, society, and politics.

Whether recounting the emergence of Free Villages, the birth of local democratic institutions, or the cultural resilience of its people, this timeline brings history to life through the years that mattered most.

Accessible, engaging, and deeply researched, The Timeline of Jamaica is a definitive reference for anyone seeking to understand the forces that gave rise to modern Jamaica.

Whether you're discovering the island's history for the first time or deepening your understanding, this book invites you to explore the years that shaped its identity.

Using This Timeline

Jamaica's history is rich and complex, shaped by centuries of migration, conquest, and transformation. Long before European contact, the island was home to the Taíno people, who arrived in waves from the Orinoco Delta in South America. They established thriving communities, leaving behind a cultural legacy still present in Jamaica today.

In 1494, Christopher Columbus first sighted Jamaica during his second voyage to the Americas. The Spanish Crown later granted the island to Columbus and his heirs, leading to Spanish colonization. However, Jamaica never became a priority for Spain due to its lack of gold, leaving it underdeveloped and lightly defended. This weakness ultimately led to England's 1655 invasion, a conquest that was neither fully planned nor immediately successful—but nonetheless changed the island's trajectory forever.

This timeline offers a chronological account of Jamaica's most pivotal events, from pre-Columbian times to modern history. Explore key moments by navigating directly to a specific year— or read sequentially to experience the full arc of Jamaica's journey from Indigenous homeland to independent nation.

TABLE OF CONTENT

— ❖ —

Hundreds of years ago, maybe even thousands, my people set forth to the sea in search of new lands. Atabey, the Goddess and Mother of all Creation, instructed Guabencex, mother of storms, volcanoes, and earthquakes, to go ahead and find and sanctify a place for the arrival of her people. Guabencex, with the might of a hurricane, went ahead and found one of the most beautiful islands she had ever seen.

She followed the land toward the rising sun and commanded it to purge itself in preparation for her people. A sacrifice needed to be made, so a small portion of the land was offered to sanctify the whole. The beauty of the island would be preserved, but a piece of it would be forever changed—a vessel of cleansing for those seeking rebirth.

The earth groaned. The heart of the island cracked open, as fire shot towards the very heavens. The fire didn't fall like rain. It flowed like rivers of liquid sun, burning everything, cleansing everything. The sand itself, once kissed by the sea, blackened and hardened—a testament to the island's sacrifice.

Atabey, who was everywhere, watched and was pleased. She called upon Yucahu, spirit of the sea and cassava, to bring forth rains that cooled the molten earth. And when the land finally rested, a new place was born; scarred, sacred, and waiting. She called it Xaymaca: land of wood and water.

— ❖ —

— from the novel The Secret Pact by Glen Carty,
a work of historical fiction

What follows is the real story

Part 1

Jamaica: Before Contact

Long before human eyes gazed upon it, the island that would become Jamaica was forged in fire and fury.

Beneath the sweltering sun stretched a wide and endless sea— a surface of shimmering beauty hiding a violent struggle below. Tectonic plates clashed and collided in a slow dance atop a sea of fire. This dance wasn't always in unison; the occasional stumble unleashed violent quakes that cracked the crust, releasing molten rock that rushed toward its fiery master —the sun.

For thousands of years, this geologic battle raged, and from it, an island was born. A central spine of mountains rose in silent majesty, dividing north from south. Along its flanks, steep ridges tumbled toward the sea. To the east, the contest had been even more intense—fiery explosions lifted the land higher still, giving rise to what we now call the Blue Mountains.

Time passed. Rain fell. Rivers carved paths through valleys. Forests took root. Birds filled the skies, and animals scurried through the underbrush. Jamaica began to breathe—a masterpiece sculpted by fire and refined by time.

...a promised land of natural beauty waiting for a people daring enough to conquer the seas.

Pre-1494

The Arawaks: Their Journey to Jamaica and the Birth of the Taíno

Generations before European ships crossed the Atlantic, the Caribbean was home to a thriving network of Indigenous peoples. Among them were the Arawaks, a sea-faring people who lived in the lush rainforests of the Orinoco River valley in northern South America. They were skilled navigators who traveled rivers and seas using various types of watercraft, with sails made from woven leaves of the moriche palm. As their communities grew, so too did their curiosity—and the need for new lands. Stories of fertile islands to the north passed down through generations spoke of a paradise beyond the horizon. Guided by these tales, they set their eyes on the sea.

With determination and expert craftsmanship, the Arawaks hollowed massive trees to build canoes capable of long ocean voyages. Traveling in groups, they began island-hopping northward through what would become the Lesser Antilles. The journey was arduous—raging storms, scorching sun, and days without sight of land tested their endurance. But they pressed on, led by knowledge of the stars, ocean currents, and the rhythms of nature.

After many days at sea, they finally spotted land on the horizon. As they approached the shores of Jamaica, they were awestruck by its beauty. The island was teeming with life, from the towering trees to the sparkling rivers. The Arawaks named their new home Xaymaca, meaning "land of wood and water".

Settling in Xaymaca

On this island, the Arawaks began a new chapter. They established villages inland and along the coasts, building circular *bohíos* (huts) with thatched roofs and creating communal plazas called *bateyes* for games, rituals, and meetings. Each village was led by a *cacique* (chief), whose larger home—the *caney*—was the center of political and ceremonial life.

They developed a harmonious way of life deeply connected to nature. Women cultivated crops like cassava, maize, sweet potatoes, and yams in carefully managed gardens called *conucos*. They skillfully processed cassava to remove its toxins and baked it into flatbread—a staple food. Men hunted small game like iguanas and birds, fished along the coasts, and even used remora fish to catch turtles. Their society was communal, balanced, and deeply tied to the rhythms of the land and sea. Tasks were divided by gender but balanced in importance. They enjoyed leisure time filled with music, dancing, storytelling, and games like *batey*, which involved a rubber ball passed between teams on the ceremonial plaza.

They believed in a dual world: one physical and one spiritual that coexisted with their own. They honored zemis—ancestral spirits and nature gods carved from stone, bone, or wood. Shamans (*behíques*) guided ceremonies that involved music, dance, ritual cleansing and offerings to these spirits. Through these practices, they sought protection, healing, and harmony.

Over time, their Arawakan culture evolved. In their Caribbean homeland, they became known as the *Taíno*, a word meaning *"the good people."* Their language, crafts, and customs reflected both their South American roots and their new island environment. The Taíno developed advanced skills in pottery, weaving, and woodworking—creating ceremonial seats (*dujos*),

3

ornaments, and tools of great beauty and utility. They adorned themselves with shells, feathers, and gold jewelry during festivals.

A Lasting Legacy

At their height, the Taíno population in Jamaica numbered in the tens of thousands. Their language gave us words still in use today—*barbacoa* (barbecue), *hamaca* (hammock), *kanoa* (canoe), and *juracán* (hurricane). Their story is not only one of survival and adaptation, but of a vibrant civilization rooted in harmony with nature.

But their peaceful way of life would not endure forever.

In 1494, foreign sails appeared on the horizon. The arrival of Christopher Columbus marked the beginning of a dramatic and often tragic transformation—not only for the Taíno of Jamaica, but for Indigenous cultures throughout the Caribbean.

Their story, however, lives on—in the land, in language, and in the enduring spirit of the Jamaican people.

Part 2

1494 – 1654: The Age of Exploration and Spanish Colonization

Jamaica's recorded history begins with Christopher Columbus's arrival in 1494, marking the start of over 150 years of Spanish rule. During this period, the island was transformed into a colonial outpost, serving as a strategic supply station for Spanish fleets. However, lacking the gold wealth of other Spanish territories, Jamaica remained underdeveloped. The forced labor of the Taíno people and the later introduction of African slaves under the encomienda system defined early colonial life. The Spanish neglect of the island, coupled with increasing English aggression in the Caribbean, set the stage for a major turning point in 1655, when England wrested control from Spain.

1494

Christopher Columbus sighted Jamaica.

The logs from Columbus's second voyage, which led to the discovery of Jamaica, have been lost; however, fragments and secondary accounts provide insights. As a result, most of what we know comes from indirect references and firsthand accounts written by others who were onboard. The most reliable sources include *Historia de los Reyes Católicos by Andrés Bernáldez*, a Spanish priest and historian who served as chaplain to the Archbishop of Seville, Diego Deza. Bernáldez had access to important figures of the time, including Columbus himself, and his work was written after discussions with the explorer. It is believed that Historia may have drawn from Columbus's original logs, now lost. Other important sources include *Historie (Historia del Almirante)*, written by Columbus's son Fernando, and *De Orbe Novo Decades by Peter Martyr*, a historian of Spanish explorations and chaplain to the court of King Ferdinand II of Aragon and Queen Isabella I of Castile.

One of the earliest descriptions of Jamaica appears in Bernáldez's Historia de los Reyes Católicos, in which Columbus is quoted as saying:

> *"...the most beautiful island that eyes ever saw. The country is most mountainous and it seems as if the earth was touching the sky. The inhabitants have more canoes than those of any other islands thereabouts, and the largest so far seen, all made in one piece out of the trunk of a tree."*

As Columbus approached the island, approximately 60 canoes filled with Indigenous people paddled out to meet his ships.

Most retreated when they realized the vessels would not stop, but a few brave individuals came alongside. Columbus's crew offered them gifts, including clothing and trinkets. The ships anchored at a location Columbus named Santa Gloria, inspired by the extreme beauty of the surrounding landscape, which he likened to Spain's famed gardens of Valencia.

The following morning, in search of a harbor to repair their ships, Columbus and his fleet sailed about four leagues west (approximately 13.5 miles) before finding a suitable location. As a small party was dispatched to inspect the entrance of the harbor, they were attacked by Indigenous warriors in two canoes, hurling arrows and spears. The attack was repelled, and Columbus decided that a show of strength was necessary to prevent further resistance. He ordered three boats to shore, where his men fired upon the Indigenous people, wounding several and forcing the rest to retreat.

Bernáldez describes the aftermath:

> "...and then he saw so many Indians that the earth was covered with them, all painted in a thousand colors, but the greatest number in black, and all of them naked as it was their custom, with plumes on their heads in various manners and the chest and stomach covered with palm leaves. They shouted and screamed in the loudest manner and threw spears which did not reach the vessels."

Recognizing the urgent need for water and wood for repairs, Columbus calculated that he needed to assert his dominance. He ordered three boats to land, where his crew reportedly fired crossbows at the Indigenous warriors, wounding many and forcing the rest to flee.

The reaction of the warriors to the attack is described as follows:

> "...they discharged their crossbows at them and when the Indians found they hurt they begun to be afraid; then the crews on the three

boats jumped on the shore and continued shooting at the Indians, who, on seeing this, ran away in such fright that there was not a man or woman left in the neighborhood. A dog that was landed from one of the caravels followed the Indians, biting and hurting them very much for a dog is as good as ten men against the Indians."

The next morning, a group of six Indigenous men returned, offering gifts. Columbus, pleased with their gesture of peace, befriended them. For the remainder of his stay, he was given everything he needed in abundance.

Alternate Accounts and Interpretations

While Bernáldez offers one of the most vivid descriptions of Columbus's arrival, other accounts from the period present slightly different versions of the events—particularly regarding the location of the landing and the interactions that followed.

Fernando Columbus, in his Historie, presents an alternative sequence. According to his account, the party that was attacked while inspecting the harbor entrance chose to retreat rather than engage in conflict. Columbus initially sailed away but later reconsidered, realizing he needed to assert his strength to deter further hostilities. He then sailed to a horseshoe-shaped harbor, which he named Puerto Bueno, where he ordered his men to fire crossbows at the Indigenous people who had gathered on the shore, wounding six or seven. The next day, the Indigenous people returned with offerings. Columbus accepted the gesture, and for the rest of his time there, he was given what he needed to repair his ships.

On May 9, 1494, Columbus sailed west along the northern coast of Jamaica. Unable to continue due to unfavorable winds, he eventually set a course back to Cuba.

Historians generally agree that the site where Columbus first landed, Santa Gloria, is in St. Ann's Bay, near Seville. This conclusion is based on descriptions in historical texts, geographic clues, and Columbus's known route along Jamaica's north coast. Meanwhile, the location where he repaired his ships, Puerto Bueno, is believed to be Discovery Bay, approximately 14 miles to the west.

The Core of the Contradiction:

The contradiction lies in the sequence and location of events — specifically:

Bernáldez's account suggests that Columbus first landed at Santa Gloria (widely accepted to be St. Ann's Bay), and from there, moved west in search of a harbor to repair his ships.

Fernando Columbus, in Historie, does not explicitly mention Santa Gloria. Instead, he describes the incident of the hostile encounter and ship repair happening at a horseshoe-shaped harbor he calls Puerto Bueno — believed to be Discovery Bay.

The Implication:

If we go by Fernando's version alone, it might imply that Puerto Bueno was the initial landing site, since he doesn't mention Santa Gloria at all.

But Bernáldez clearly places Santa Gloria as the first point of landfall, and this is supported by most modern historians, especially since it later became the site of Seville, the first Spanish settlement.

So the contradiction is not necessarily that the two authors directly disagree, but that Fernando omits Santa Gloria, which leads to ambiguity. His account could be interpreted as suggesting that Puerto Bueno was the main or only stop, while

Bernáldez presents a more sequential narrative: first Santa Gloria, then Puerto Bueno for repairs.

Incidentally, Columbus returned to Puerto Bueno during his fourth voyage, when he was stranded in Jamaica—further cementing the harbor's importance in his explorations.

Scholarly Interpretation:

Most historians resolve this by treating Santa Gloria (St. Ann's Bay) as the first landing site, followed shortly by a move westward to Puerto Bueno (Discovery Bay) for ship repairs. The contradiction is resolved not by proving one source wrong, but by synthesizing both into a probable timeline of events.

Columbus's Motivation for Seeking Jamaica

Fernando's account also sheds light on why Columbus sought out Jamaica in the first place. He had heard from Indigenous people on other islands that Jamaica was rich in gold. However, no gold was ever found. This turned out to be a critical factor in the island's history. Unlike Hispaniola, which was heavily colonized due to its mineral wealth, Jamaica did not attract much attention from the Spanish Crown. As a result, the island remained underdeveloped and lightly defended, making it far easier for the English to conquer it a century and a half later.

1503

Columbus Shipwrecked in Jamaica

Christopher Columbus embarked on his fourth and final voyage on May 9, 1502, departing from Cádiz, Spain. This journey would prove to be one of his most disastrous. After a year of hardships—including severe storms, dwindling supplies, and hostile encounters with Indigenous peoples—two of his ships had to be abandoned along the coast of Panama. The remaining vessels, La Capitana and Vizcaíno, were barely seaworthy, their hulls riddled with holes from shipworms, a common maritime threat in tropical waters.

By June 24, 1503, the ailing 52-year-old Columbus and his weary crew reached the northern coast of Jamaica, near the site he had first visited in 1494. With no means of repairing the vessels and his fleet falling apart, Columbus and his men were effectively stranded on the island.

It was during this period, while seeking aid and attempting to maintain contact with the Spanish monarchy, that Columbus wrote a letter vividly describing both his circumstances and his interpretation of the lands he had encountered. **Importantly, Columbus still believed he was sailing along the eastern fringes of Asia.**

From the outset, Columbus's goal had not been to discover a new continent, but to find a westward sea route to Asia—specifically the rich trading centers of India, Japan (Cipangu), and Cathay, the European name for northern China. The known route to Asia required a long and treacherous journey around the Horn of Africa, which he hoped to bypass entirely. Relying on flawed maps and underestimating the Earth's true size, Columbus remained convinced—even after multiple voyages—that the Caribbean islands he had reached were part of mainland Asia.

In the 1503 letter excerpted below, written during the final leg of his fourth voyage, Columbus refers to the province of Mago, which he believed bordered Cathay. In doing so, he identifies

Cuba as part of northern China. The letter also captures the severe conditions that led him to Jamaica, where he and his crew would remain stranded for over a year before rescue.

An excerpt from the letter:

On the thirteenth of May I reached the province of Mago, which borders on Cathay , and thence I started for the island of Española [ed. — the name he gave Hispaniola on his first voyage]. I sailed two days with a good wind, after which it became contrary. The route that I followed called forth all my care to avoid the numerous islands, that I might not be stranded on the shoals that lie in their neighborhood. The sea was very tempestuous, and I was driven backward under bare poles. I anchored at an island, where I lost, at one stroke, three anchors; and, at midnight, when the weather was such that the world appeared to be coming to an end, the cables of the other ship broke, and it came down upon my vessel with such force that it was a wonder we were not dashed to pieces; the single anchor that remained to me was, next to the Lord, our only preservation.

After six days, when the weather became calm, I resumed my journey, having already lost all my tackle; my ships were pierced by borers more than a honey-comb and the crew entirely paralyzed with fear and in despair. I reached the island a little beyond the point at which I first arrived at it, and there I turned in to recover myself after the storm; but I afterwards put into a much safer port in the same island.

After eight days I put to sea again, and reached Jamaica by the end of June; but always beating against contrary winds, and with the ships in the worst possible condition. With three pumps, and the use of pots and kettles, we could scarcely clear the water that came into the ship, there being no remedy but this for the mischief done by the ship-worm.
—Excerpt from Columbus's Fourth Voyage, translated in The Northmen, Columbus and Cabot, 985–1503 (1906).

With no other option, Columbus's men beached the ships in a sheltered cove along the coast of St. Ann, where they would remain for over a year.

Desperate for rescue, on July 17, 1503, Columbus sent two of his most trusted captains—Diego Méndez and Bartolomeo Fieschi—on a dangerous canoe voyage to Hispaniola, accompanied by Indigenous Taíno paddlers. The mission was clear: seek help from Governor Nicolás de Ovando y Cáceres in Santo Domingo. However, Ovando reportedly harbored deep resentment toward Columbus and deliberately delayed assistance, leaving the stranded crew to fend for themselves.

1504

Columbus Rescued from Jamaica

As months passed without news from Méndez and Fieschi, tensions between Columbus's crew and the Indigenous Taíno population began to escalate. Initially, the Taíno supplied food to Columbus's men, but as the months dragged on, they grew tired of supporting the stranded Spaniards, whose demands increased. Starvation loomed.

Realizing that maintaining the goodwill of the Taíno was essential for survival, Columbus devised a bold deception.

Armed with knowledge from astronomical charts, he predicted a lunar eclipse would occur on February 29, 1504. Seizing the moment, Columbus gathered the Taíno Caciques (chiefs) and made a dire proclamation.

The event was recorded in the book *The Life of the Admiral Christopher Columbus (La Historia del Almirante Don*

Cristóbal Colón) written by his son, Fernando Columbus:

The day before the eclipse, the chiefs having arrived, the Admiral addressed the gathering through an interpreter. He explained that we were Christians who believed in God, who lives in Heaven, and that we were His servants. God, he said, rewarded the good and punished the wicked.

As for the Indians, God was very angry with them for neglecting to bring us food, which we paid for by barter. In His anger, God had determined to punish them with famine and pestilence. To convince the incredulous, God would send them a clear token from Heaven of the punishment they were about to receive.

The Admiral warned them to observe the moon that night. She would rise inflamed with wrath, signifying the chastisement God would visit upon them.

Having spoken, the Admiral dismissed the gathering. The Indians departed, some frightened by his words, while others scoffed at his threats.

But at the rising of the moon, the eclipse began, and the higher it rose, the more complete the eclipse became. The Indians grew so frightened that, with great howling and lamentation, they came running from all directions to the ships, laden with provisions, and begged the Admiral to intercede with God so that He might not vent His wrath upon them. They promised to diligently supply all the Spaniards' needs in the future.

The Admiral replied that he wished to speak briefly with his God and retired to his cabin while the eclipse waxed, and the Indians cried all the while for his help. When the Admiral perceived that the crescent phase of the moon was finishing and that it would soon shine forth clearly, he emerged from his cabin, saying that he had appealed to his God and prayed for them. He declared that he had promised God, on their behalf, that henceforth they would be good and treat the Christians well, providing provisions and all else they needed.

God had now pardoned them, he proclaimed, and in token of this, they would soon see the moon's anger and inflammation pass away.

When the Indians saw his words coming true, they offered many thanks to the Admiral and praised his God as long as the eclipse continued.

From that time forward, they were diligent in providing the Spaniards with all they needed and spoke loudly in praise of the Christian God. For they believed that eclipses were very harmful, and, being ignorant of their cause and regular recurrence, and unaware that men on Earth could predict the sky's events, they were certain that the Admiral's God had revealed the eclipse to him.
— Source: The Life of the Admiral Christopher Columbus by His Son Fernando

The ruse worked. The Taínos believed Columbus had supernatural power and immediately resumed supplying food. This event became one of the most famous uses of celestial knowledge in European-Indigenous encounters.

How Columbus Knew About the Eclipse

It is widely believed that the astronomical almanac Columbus consulted was the "Ephemerides" by Johannes Müller, a German astronomer also known by his Latinized name Regiomontanus. This popular almanac contained detailed predictions of celestial events, including eclipses, and was frequently used by European navigators.

However, the exact source Columbus relied on remains uncertain. Some historians suggest he may have consulted additional charts or received guidance from court astronomers. Navigators often used a combination of resources, cross-referencing predictions from different almanacs to ensure accuracy. With access to Spanish and Portuguese maritime knowledge, Columbus likely drew from various materials.

Regardless of the specific source, Columbus's use of astronomical knowledge was a strategic move. By forewarning the Taíno of the impending lunar eclipse on February 29, 1504, he successfully manipulated their beliefs, presenting the event as a divine sign and securing their continued cooperation during his stranded stay in Jamaica.

Columbus is Rescued

Diego Méndez finally returned to Jamaica on June 29, 1504, after successfully securing approval for a rescue ship. The rescue vessel arrived on August 13, taking Columbus and his remaining men to Hispaniola. On November 7, 1504, Columbus finally set sail back to Spain, arriving in Sanlúcar de Barrameda—only to find that Queen Isabella, his greatest patron, was on her deathbed.

Exhausted, frail, and politically weakened, Columbus would never sail again. He died in 1506, convinced until his last breath that he had reached the fringes of Asia.

1506

Columbus's Death Sparks a Legal Battle

Christopher Columbus died on May 20, 1506, in Valladolid, Spain, at the age of 54. Though once the most celebrated explorer of his time, Columbus spent his final years in relative obscurity, embroiled in legal disputes over the wealth and titles he had once been granted by the Spanish Crown. His passing marked the beginning of a bitter, decades-long legal battle led by his son Diego Columbus to restore the family's lost privileges in the New World.

Diego Columbus: The Fight for Recognition

When Columbus embarked on his second voyage in 1493, his son Diego Columbus was appointed as a page at the Spanish court, where he was groomed for a position of influence. As his expeditions continued, Columbus was granted a series of titles, including Viceroy, Governor, and Admiral of the Ocean Sea. However, his declining fortunes and political conflicts with Spanish officials led to these honors being gradually stripped.

Following his father's death, Diego launched an aggressive legal campaign against the Spanish Crown to reclaim what he saw as his family's rightful legacy. By this time, Diego had married María Álvarez de Toledo, the cousin of King Ferdinand II of Aragon, giving him direct access to the royal court. This alliance provided him with a degree of influence, but it would take years of persistent legal challenges before he achieved any success.

1508-1511

In **1508**, Diego was appointed Governor of the Indies, and one of his first actions was to order the settlement of Jamaica. He tasked Juan de Esquivel, a seasoned Spanish conquistador, with leading the colonization effort before Diego personally arrived in Santo Domingo in July **1509** to assume direct control of Spanish territories in the Caribbean. However, this was not enough—Diego sought all the titles and privileges his father had once held, including Viceroy of the Indies.

In **1511**, the Crown partially relented, granting him the hereditary title of Viceroy of the Islands. However, this title held significantly less authority than the full Viceroyalty of the Indies that his father had once possessed, as the Crown sought to prevent the consolidation of power. This left Diego in a constant struggle to reclaim his family's lost influence.

1526 - Diego Dies, Leaving an Unsettled Dispute

Despite his efforts, Diego Columbus died in 1526 before the legal battle over his family's claims could be fully settled. Over the years, he had made multiple trips to Spain, lobbying for the restoration of his father's titles and privileges, but his ambitions remained unfulfilled at the time of his death.

1536 - The Dispute Is Finally Resolved and the Family Inherits Jamaica

After Diego's death, his widow, María Álvarez de Toledo, continued the fight on behalf of their children, determined to secure their inheritance. For a decade, she pursued relentless legal challenges, refusing to let the family's claims go unanswered. At last, a final compromise was reached in June 1536.

—See 1536 *for how the legal battle was ultimately resolved.*

1508

Diego Columbus & the Settlement of Jamaica (Colony of Santiago)

While engaged in legal battles in Spain, Diego Columbus was appointed Governor of the Indies in 1508, following years of lobbying for the recognition of his father's legacy. One of his first acts was to establish a formal Spanish settlement in Jamaica, an island that had previously served only as a supply station.

He appointed Juan de Esquivel, a Spanish conquistador who had accompanied Columbus in 1494, as his lieutenant. Esquivel landed at Santa Gloria (St. Ann's Bay) with 80 settlers and their families to establish the first European colony on the island.

The settlement, Sevilla la Nueva (New Seville), was built near the Taíno village of Maima. The Spanish later renamed it Sevilla d'Oro (Golden Seville) in anticipation of gold deposits, though none were ever found. The gold ornaments worn by the Taíno people had led the Spanish to believe that the island was rich in the precious metal, an idea that persisted for centuries—later English settlers would speak of the "King of Spain's secret gold mines."

However, Sevilla la Nueva never flourished. Disease, food shortages, and conflicts with the Taíno people made it difficult for the Spanish to maintain control. By the 1530s, Spain had all but abandoned Jamaica, focusing instead on wealthier colonies like Mexico and Peru.

1511

Spanish Settlers Permitted to Use Taínos for Labor

By 1511, Spanish settlers in Jamaica had realized that the island lacked the rich gold deposits found in other parts of the Spanish Empire. Juan de Esquivel, the first Spanish governor of Jamaica, reported to the Crown that no significant gold reserves existed, leading Spain to shift its focus to more lucrative colonies in Cuba, Hispaniola, and South America.

In response, the Spanish monarchy encouraged settlers to use the Taíno people as a labor force to sustain the colony and supply provisions for Spanish expeditions elsewhere in the Caribbean. Settlers were granted encomiendas—land allotments that included the right to use Taíno labor for mining, construction, transportation, and farming. Typical grants ranged from 150 to 200 Indigenous workers per settler.

The absence of gold diminished Jamaica's strategic importance in the Spanish Empire. Fewer settlers arrived, and colonial development slowed. Unlike Cuba and Hispaniola, which became hubs of Spanish power in the Americas, Jamaica remained lightly defended and underdeveloped, a weakness that would later make it vulnerable to foreign invasion.

1517

The First African Slaves in Jamaica

In 1517, the first African slaves were brought to Jamaica by the Spanish. These individuals did not arrive directly from Africa; rather, they were Africans or the descendants of Africans who had already been enslaved in Spain.

The importation of enslaved Africans into Spanish territories had begun earlier. In 1501, King Ferdinand of Spain authorized the governor of Hispaniola to import black slaves born under Christian rule, believing they would be more "reliable" than newly enslaved Indigenous people. This decree marked the first recorded instance of Europeans transporting African slaves across the Atlantic to the New World.

Excerpt of the letter from the Spanish Monarchs to The Governor of Hispaniola:

Because with great care we have procured the conversion of the Indians to our Holy Catholic Faith, and furthermore, if there are still people there who are doubtful of the faith in their own conversions, it would be a hindrance [to them], and therefore we will not permit, nor allow to go there [to the Americas] Moors nor Jews nor heretics nor reconciled heretics, nor persons who are recently converted to our faith, except if they are black slaves, or other slaves, that have been born under the dominion of our natural Christian subjects.
—Source: *New Iberian World: A Documentary History of the Discovery and Settlement of Latin America to the Early 17th Century, Vol. II*, ed. by John H. Parry and Robert G. Keith.

Spain's justification for the enslavement of Africans in the New World was based on religious and economic motives. The monarchy saw them as a necessary labor force for supporting its expanding empire, particularly as the Taíno population declined due to disease, harsh treatment, and overwork under Spanish rule.

1518

New Seville, the First Capital of Jamaica and the First Slaves direct from Africa

In 1518, the Spanish Governor of Jamaica, Francisco de Garay, ordered the relocation of Sevilla la Nueva (New Seville), the island's first capital, closer to the coastline. The original settlement had been established in the Taíno village of Maima, but the Spanish sought a more accessible location for trade, defense, and agriculture.

The new settlement occupied a fertile alluvial plain that

extended from the northern coastline to the limestone highlands further inland. Today, the site remains historically significant for three key reasons:

- It was Jamaica's first capital under Spanish rule.
- It became one of the earliest sites in the region to receive a steady flow of enslaved Africans.
- It later became the location of the post-1655 British sugar plantation known as Seville, which today is one of Jamaica's most important archaeological sites, offering insights into the island's colonial, African, and Taíno heritage.

By 1525, Sevilla had developed into a small but structured colony. The settlement included a stone fortress, a Franciscan monastery, a sugar factory, and an artist workshop, making it one of the earliest examples of organized colonial urban planning in the Americas. Governor Francisco de Garay also built a castle in the settlement, reinforcing Spanish claims to the island.

The first Slaves arrive directly from Africa

In 1518, King Charles I of Spain (Ferdinand's successor) granted a four-year permit allowing an annual shipment of 4,000 enslaved Africans to be transported directly from Africa to the Spanish colonies of Hispaniola, Cuba, Jamaica, and Puerto Rico. This marked a fundamental shift in the transatlantic slave trade, as previously, most African slaves in the Spanish Caribbean had arrived indirectly from Spain or Portugal after being enslaved in Europe.

This new policy greatly increased the scale and efficiency of the slave trade, as Spanish authorities sought to replace the rapidly declining Taíno population with a labor force they deemed more resilient for plantation agriculture and construction.

By 1611, Jamaica's population had grown to approximately:

- 558 enslaved Africans*
- 107 free blacks*
- Between 1,200 and 1,400 Spaniards

This period marked the beginning of Jamaica's reliance on African slave labor, a system that would expand dramatically under British rule after their conquest of the island in 1655.

Source: Gone is the Ancient Glory, Spanish Town, Jamaica, 1551-2000 by James Roberson

---

1530

The First Jews in Jamaica

The earliest evidence of a Jewish presence in Jamaica dates back to the Spanish colonial period. Around 1530, it is highly likely that Portuguese Jewish Conversos—Jews who had been forcibly converted to Catholicism—began arriving on the island, particularly settling in Spanish Town. Their migration was a direct consequence of the intensifying religious persecution in the Iberian Peninsula, where Spain and Portugal sought to eradicate Jewish identity through forced conversions and the ruthless measures of the Inquisition.

The Iberian Inquisitions and Jewish Expulsions

The oppression of Spanish Jews had been escalating for over a century. In 1478, King Ferdinand II of Aragon and Queen Isabella I of Castile established the Spanish Inquisition, an institution controlled by the Catholic Church to root out heresy. While officially targeting non-Christians accused of secretly practicing their old faith, the Inquisition primarily became a mechanism for persecuting Jews who had converted but were suspected of maintaining Jewish customs in secret.

The situation reached its peak in 1492 when Ferdinand and Isabella issued the Alhambra Decree on March 31, expelling all Jews from Spain unless they converted to Catholicism. Given only four months to leave, thousands of Jewish families were forced to sell their possessions for a fraction of their value. Historical estimates vary, but at least 40,000 to 80,000 Jews fled Spain, with some older sources claiming numbers in the hundreds of thousands. These expelled Jews, known as Sephardim (from the Hebrew word for Spain, Sepharad), resettled in North Africa, the Ottoman Empire, and parts of Europe, forming what would become the foundation of the modern Sephardic Jewish diaspora.

The persecution did not end there. In 1497, King Manuel I of Portugal, under pressure from Spain, forcibly converted all remaining Jews in his kingdom, giving them no option to emigrate. This decree created a large population of Conversos, many of whom continued to practice their faith in secrecy, earning them the name Crypto-Jews.

Conversos and Crypto-Jews in Jamaica

Jamaica, a Spanish colony at the time, became a possible refuge for these persecuted Jews—especially those from Portugal— around the year 1530. Conversos who had been forced to embrace Catholicism likely saw Jamaica as a place where they could escape the intense scrutiny of the Iberian Inquisitions. However, religious intolerance under Spanish rule meant they had to continue outwardly living as Catholics while privately maintaining their Jewish traditions.

Jamaica's role as a haven for Conversos was limited under

Spanish rule due to the continued threat of Inquisitorial oversight, but it laid the groundwork for a more openly Jewish presence after 1655, when the British seized control of the island. The British, being more tolerant of religious minorities— especially those with valuable commercial and trading networks —allowed Sephardic Jews to settle openly in Jamaica, leading to the formal establishment of a Jewish community.

Who Were the Conversos and Crypto-Jews?

To clarify the terminology:

- Conversos – Jews who converted to Catholicism (either by force or by choice).
- Crypto-Jews – Conversos who secretly continued practicing Jewish traditions despite their official conversion.

The people arriving in Jamaica around 1530 were Conversos by definition (as they had undergone conversion), but many of them were also Crypto-Jews, maintaining their faith in secret. These were not two separate groups; rather, "Crypto-Jew" describes a subset of Conversos—those who still adhered to Jewish customs despite the threat of persecution.

Though Jamaica under Spanish rule was not a major Jewish refuge, it played a role in the survival of Jewish traditions in the New World. It was under British rule in the 17th century that Jamaica would become home to one of the earliest Jewish communities in the Caribbean, cementing its place in Sephardic Jewish history.

1534

Seville Abandoned & New Capital: Villa de la Vega (Spanish Town)

By 1534, Spanish settlers in Jamaica abandoned Sevilla la Nueva (New Seville), relocating to a new site they named Villa de la Vega (Town of the Plain). The settlement, later renamed St. Jago de la Vega and eventually Spanish Town under British rule, became Jamaica's capital and remained so until 1872, when the capital was moved to Kingston.

Motivations for Relocation

The relocation was motivated by several challenges at Sevilla la Nueva:

- Sevilla la Nueva was abandoned due to disease, food shortages, and poor conditions.
- Villa de la Vega was chosen because it was more suitable for agriculture, provided better defenses, and was centrally located for Spanish administration.

Spanish Town's location in a fertile agricultural plain made it more suitable for long-term settlement and economic development. It soon became the political and administrative center of Spanish Jamaica.

Other Spanish Settlements

- Other Spanish settlements were also established,

including:

- Esquivel (now Old Harbour Bay)
- Oristan (Bluefields)
- Savanna-la-Mar (present-day Savanna-la-Mar)
- Manterias (Montego Bay)
- Las Chorreras (Ocho Rios)
- Oracabeza (Oracabessa)
- Puerto Santa Maria (Port Maria)
- Mellila (Annotto Bay)
- Puerto Anton (Port Antonio)

Though Jamaica remained a relatively minor colony in Spain's empire, Spanish Town would serve as the island's capital for more than three centuries under both Spanish and British rule.

1536

A Final Settlement: The Columbus Family Inherits Jamaica

After a long legal battle following Christopher Columbus's death, known as the Pleitos Colombinos (Columbus Lawsuits), his son, Diego Columbus, won partial recognition of his family's claims in 1511. The Crown granted him the hereditary title of Viceroy of the Islands, a position that included oversight of territories like Jamaica. However, this title came with limited authority compared to the sweeping powers his father had once held. While Diego served as the official governor of Jamaica under the Spanish Crown, his ambitions for full control remained unmet.

Despite this partial victory, the legal disputes continued. Diego pressed for greater authority, but his efforts ended with his death in 1526, leaving the matter unresolved.

Determined to secure her children's inheritance, María Álvarez de Toledo, Diego's widow, took up the legal fight. As a member of the influential Toledo family and cousin to King Ferdinand II, María wielded significant court influence. For another decade, she pursued the family's claims, refusing to accept the diminished legacy left to her children.

At last, in June 1536, a final compromise was reached between the Crown and the Columbus family. Rather than restoring the full rights Diego had sought, the Spanish Crown offered a settlement to his son, Luis Columbus. Under its terms, Luis was granted:

- A perpetual annuity of 10,000 ducats
- The island of Jamaica as a personal fief
- A 25-square-league estate (85 square miles) on the Isthmus of Panama
- The noble titles of Duke of Veragua and Marquis of Jamaica

However, even this settlement came with restrictions. While Luis Columbus held Jamaica as a personal possession, he was forbidden from fortifying the island without the direct permission of the Spanish King. This restriction weakened the island's defenses, contributing to Britain's relatively easy conquest of Jamaica in 1655.

Conflicting Accounts on Resolution

The 1536 settlement undeniably conferred noble titles on Luis, including the hereditary titles of Duke of Veragua and Marquis of Jamaica, along with financial compensation. However, whether Jamaica itself was fully transferred to the family's control at that time or merely in name remains uncertain. Some scholars point to 1557 as the moment when Philip II, after revising previous agreements, formalized the transfer of Jamaica under plenary dominion, granting Luis full legal authority to govern the island, manage its resources, and exercise control over its inhabitants.

he 1536 settlement undeniably conferred noble titles on Luis, including the hereditary titles of Duke of Veragua and Marquis of Jamaica, along with financial compensation. While it remains unclear whether Jamaica itself was formally transferred at this point or later in 1557, the titles reflect the family's growing recognition and authority over the island.

—See 1557 - A Reassessment of the Columbus Family's Inheritance

---

1557

A Reassessment of the Columbus Family's Inheritance

While the settlement of 1536 awarded Luis Colón noble titles and financial compensation, some accounts indicate that his actual control over Jamaica did not materialize until 1557. Following a reassessment under Philip II, the Crown reclaimed the Veragua estate and Santo Domingo properties, which had proven difficult for Luis to govern.

In exchange, Jamaica was granted to Luis in plenary dominion — meaning he held the island with full authority, though still under Spanish sovereignty. This adjustment gave him formal control over the island's administration, trade, and internal affairs. Despite this, the Crown retained oversight by forbidding any fortifications without royal approval — a vulnerability that would have consequences during the English invasion of 1655.

One historical account describes the development as follows:

> *"Twenty years after the last-mentioned arrangement, and when it had but just begun to take effect, another modification was made, in the reign of Philip II. (A. D. 1557). The Veragua property and that which was granted in Santo Domingo were taken back by the crown, and in their place D. Luis Colon received the island of Jamaica, in plenary dominion, with the title of Marquis of Jamaica."*
> *—From "The Family of Columbus", published in the American Historical Review (via JSTOR)*

Although Luis retained his noble titles of Duke of Veragua and Marquis of Jamaica, Jamaica was likely viewed as a replacement holding intended to maintain the family's noble standing. This final adjustment marked the conclusion of the Columbus family's legal battle. However, the restrictions on fortifications remained in place, leaving Jamaica exposed — a weakness the English would later exploit.

—See 1536 - A Final Settlement for further context on the original settlement.

English Attacks: Sir Anthony Shirley's Raid on Jamaica

By the late 1500s, Spanish Jamaica was poorly defended and vulnerable to foreign attacks. In 1597, Francisco Hernandez, presbyter and canon of Jamaica's Holy Church of Xamayca, described the island as a place of hardship. The Spanish population was small, many of whom lived in poverty. The colony's economy revolved around cassava, hides, and meat, which were shipped to Havana and other Spanish settlements.

The Arrival of the English Fleet

During this period, English and French privateers frequently attacked Spanish ships and coastal settlements. In February 1597, an English fleet of seven ships—four large warships and three smaller launches—sailed along Jamaica's south coast, searching for Passage Fort, the main entrance to the island's principal port. Unaware of its exact location, the fleet first sailed west to Negril Point before realizing their mistake. They then doubled back eastward, eventually finding the correct landing point near Passage Fort, close to modern-day Portmore.

The Invasion of Villa de la Vega (Spanish Town)

Leaving the larger ships anchored offshore, about 200-300 English troops landed on February 4, 1597, and began marching seven miles inland toward Villa de la Vega (Spanish Town). The Spanish governor, Licentiate Francisco de Nabeda Albarado, initially gathered citizens to defend the town but quickly recognized the futility of resistance. Facing overwhelming numbers, he ordered an evacuation, and the settlers fled into the interior jungle, carrying whatever valuables they could.

The English Demand a Ransom

The English were met by a Taíno guide named Pedro, who led them to the now-deserted town. General Sir Anthony Shirley sent a messenger to the Spanish governor, demanding:

- 1,000 arrobas (approx. 25,000 lbs) of meat.
- 400 cargas (pack loads) of cassava.

If the demands were not met, Shirley threatened to destroy the town.

Upon receiving the ultimatum, Governor Nabeda sought counsel from church officials who had taken refuge in a place known as Cayo de la Legua (no modern location by that name is known to exist today). Abbott Don Francisco Marques de Villalobos, along with Dominican friars, argued that paying the ransom would only encourage future attacks. They decided no one would assist the English, imposing a death penalty on anyone caught aiding them.

Destruction of Spanish Town

After waiting a week with no response, the English grew impatient and furious. They burned approximately 60 buildings and raided plantations destroying them in the process.

Shirley, furious at the abbott's defiance, ordered his men to hunt down the clergy.

Guided again by Pedro, the English forces located the clergy's hideout, ransacked the camp, and looted all valuables. One witness described how the English took everything—clothing, supplies, even the wool from mattresses—leaving nothing but broken chests and debris.

When the Spanish town accountant, Pedro de Castillo, heard of the attack, he urged the clergy to take refuge on his plantation at Maimón.

The Governor Negotiates a Peace

Facing the futility of further resistance, Governor Nabeda authorized Treasurer Francisco Arnaldo to negotiate with General Shirley. They reached a deal:

- The Spanish would supply meat, cassava, carts, and horses.
- In return, Shirley would cease hostilities.

To seal the agreement, Captain Francisco Bejarano carried Shirley's signet ring as proof of the truce. After 40 days, the English departed Jamaica with the supplies, carts, horses, and whatever plunder they had gathered.

The Lasting Impact of Shirley's Raid

Though Shirley's forces never intended to seize Jamaica permanently, the raid exposed Spain's weak defenses. Fifty-eight years later, when Oliver Cromwell's fleet failed to conquer Hispaniola in 1655, Jamaica was chosen as an alternative target. The intelligence gathered from raids like Shirley's likely influenced that decision—proving that Jamaica was vulnerable, underdeveloped, and poorly defended.

—*Primary Source: "The Spanish Version of Sir Anthony Shirley's Raid of Jamaica, 1597" by Don Fernando Melgarejo De Cordova (1922), based on unpublished documents from the Archivo General de Indias, Seville, Spain.*

1643

Captain William Jackson's Raid on Spanish Jamaica

In 1643, Captain William Jackson, an English privateer operating under a commission from Robert Rich, the 2nd Earl of Warwick, led an expedition to raid Spanish holdings in the Caribbean. The Earl of Warwick was a leading figure in England's navy and a key supporter of Parliament during the English Civil War. His sponsorship of privateering ventures like Jackson's aligned with England's broader strategy of challenging Spanish dominance in the Americas.

At the time, Spain controlled vast portions of the Caribbean and had established a monopoly on trade and valuable resources in the region. England, eager to weaken Spanish power and expand its own influence, increasingly turned to privateers—state-sanctioned pirates—to harass Spanish colonies and disrupt their economic stronghold. Jackson's mission was part of this larger effort to break Spanish control and secure a foothold for England in the West Indies.

Jackson's Attack on Jamaica

Jackson's fleet set sail from England and, after raiding several Spanish territories, arrived off the coast of Jamaica in October 1643. He anchored near Passage Fort, close to St. Jago de la Vega (Spanish Town), the capital of Spanish Jamaica. With a force of about 500 men, Jackson launched an assault on the town. The Spanish defenders, caught off guard, offered little resistance, and the English easily seized control.

Ransom and Withdrawal

Rather than occupying the island permanently, Jackson opted to ransack the town and extort a ransom from the Spanish authorities. He demanded a substantial sum of money and supplies in exchange for sparing the settlement from further destruction. The Spanish, recognizing their limited ability to resist, agreed to pay Jackson 7,000 pieces of eight (Spanish silver coins), along with cattle and provisions.

Having secured his spoils, Jackson and his men withdrew from Jamaica, leaving it under Spanish control. However, his raid—like others before it—exposed the island's vulnerabilities, revealing poor defenses and providing valuable intelligence on the southern coast. This knowledge would later influence Oliver Cromwell's Western Design in 1655, when England returned with a full-scale invasion to seize the island from Spain.

Long-Term Significance

Though Jackson's raid did not result in immediate territorial gains for England, it played a role in shaping the nation's long-term ambitions in the Caribbean. While England's eyes were set on Hispaniola, the raid provided valuable intelligence, revealing Jamaica's weak defenses. This knowledge would resurface a little over a decade later, contributing to the decision to seize the island during Cromwell's Western Design.

1654

The Anglo-Spanish War & Cromwell's Western Design

In his book, Growth of English Industry and Commerce (1890), historian William Cunningham observed that sixteenth, seventeenth, and much of eighteenth-century English politicians shared a common goal: to increase England's power relative to other nations—by any means necessary. They believed national strength depended on:

- The accumulation of treasure
- The development of shipping
- The maintenance of an effective population

This philosophy likely shaped Oliver Cromwell's worldview when he rose to power in 1649, the same year King Charles I was executed, paving the way for Cromwell to become Lord Protector of England. With control over England, Scotland, and Ireland, Cromwell turned his ambitions toward breaking Spain's dominance in the Americas.

The Western Design: A Plan to Seize Spanish America

By the mid-1600s, global commerce had expanded dramatically due to Spain's New World colonies. Cromwell saw an opportunity to disrupt Spain's monopoly and increase England's wealth and influence. His strategy, known as the Western Design, aimed to:

- Capture Hispaniola (Spain's most prized Caribbean

possession)

- Attack and weaken Spanish colonies
- Expand England's control in the West Indies

In December 1654, Cromwell dispatched a powerful naval force to the Caribbean under the command of General Robert Venables and Admiral William Penn (father of William Penn, founder of Pennsylvania).

Their Mission: seize Hispaniola for England and establish a foothold in Spanish America.

The Result: A failed attack on Hispaniola, Jamaica is captured and the start of the 1654-1660 Anglo-Spanish war.

Part 3

1655 – 1699: English Conquest and the Rise of Sugar and Slavery

With the English conquest of Jamaica in 1655, the island entered a period of transformation. Initially a struggling colony reliant on privateering, it soon developed into a major center of sugar production. The late 17th century saw the expansion of plantation agriculture, driven by the transatlantic slave trade and the Royal African Company. Port Royal flourished as the "wickedest city on earth," thriving on piracy and trade, but its dominance faded with the 1692 earthquake. Meanwhile, the increasing number of enslaved Africans led to growing resistance, laying the foundation for future struggles.

1655

England Conquers Jamaica from Spain

After a disastrous failed assault on Hispaniola, English commanders General Robert Venables and Admiral William Penn feared returning to England empty-handed. Instead, they turned their sights on Jamaica, an island known to be weakly defended—a fact likely gathered from previous English incursions, including Sir Anthony Shirley's raid in 1597 and Captain William Jackson's attack in 1643.

In May 1655, the English fleet landed at Passage Fort, near the capital Villa de la Vega (later Spanish Town). The Spanish forces, caught off guard and outnumbered, were quickly overwhelmed, and the island was formally claimed for England. However, the conquest was far from complete. Spanish forces, aided by escaped African slaves under Spanish rule (the early Maroons), retreated into the mountains and the north coast, launching a prolonged guerrilla resistance that would last five more years.

Eyewitness Accounts: The Hardships of English Occupation

Much of what we know about Jamaica's conquest and early English rule comes from The Narrative of General Venables, a collection of letters and reports from the expedition, edited by historian C.H. Firth for the Royal Historical Society in 1900.

These firsthand accounts paint a grim picture of English occupation in 1655. Despite their initial success in seizing the island, English forces quickly found themselves in dire conditions, facing:

- Spanish guerrilla attacks
- A lack of food and supplies
- Rampant disease that decimated their ranks

By November 1655, the English garrison was so weakened by illness and starvation that they were forced to eat whatever they could find, including dogs and horses. The dead were buried in shallow graves, only to be dug up by dogs and eaten, further demoralizing the surviving troops. Their challenges are described in the following excerpt from the General's letters.

Language of the Original Text

The following excerpt from The Narrative of General Venables, written sometime before May 7, 1677, have been lightly edited for readability. Original language and spelling (including typos) have been preserved where possible. Passages where the exact meaning is unclear have been left as written.

Examples of changes:

Original: "...it was agreed that the Spaniard should come in that day sennight out of the woods where they then lay, and bring in all their armes..."

Modified: "...it was agreed that the Spaniards should come out of the woods in a week where they would then lay down their arms..." ["sennight" is old english for in the space of seven nights and days]

Original: "the Generall, Vice Admirall, and Rere Admirall shott severall guns at his funerall."

Modified: the General, Vice Admiral, and Rear Admiral shot several guns at his funeral.

Original: ...we saw Jamaica Iland ...our souldiers in number 7000 (the sea regiment being none of them)

Modified: ...we saw Jamaica Iland ...our soldiers in number 7,000 (excluding the naval force)

—Excerpt begins: Taken directly from the text, with minor edits for readability.

The following picks up from the ending of the account of the failed mission in Hispaniola where the English forces were near decimated and now totally defeated, they sail away from Hispaniola with their sight on Jamaica.

Letters about the English Conquest of Jamaica in 1655
From The Narrative of General Venables, written late 1600s.

I

On Saturday the 5 of May, the fleet stood away for the Island of Jamaica. On Tuesday we saw the Island of Navasa like a small bowling green [ed.—a small uninhabited reef island with an abandoned lighthouse located northeast of Jamaica, south of Cuba, west of Haiti], when Commissary Winslow, died, and was thrown overboard; the General, Vice Admiral, and Rear Admiral shot several guns at his funeral.

On Wednesday morning, being the 9th, of May, we saw Jamaica Island, very high land afar off.

Thursday the 10th, our soldiers in number 7,000 (excluding the naval force) landed at the 3 forts, or rather breastworks [ed.—temporary fortification about breast high], about the point, [in] which there were 8 pieces of ordinance, but only 3 were mounted, which took about 20 shots at us; the enemy had about 300 men, likewise resisting with a few shots, all missing our men, who seeing that our men were sure to land, leapt to the middle in water and abandoned the forts; the Martin galley [a ship of war] quickly gaining upon the Spaniards under whose guns we landed.

These 3 forts, or rather breastwork, were very strong and cannon proof; from these forts our men marched through a savannah to the highway in a wood leading to the town, where about half a mile farther, there was another breastwork for cannon and musketeers, which without resistance we passed, and within a little mile of the town, which lay 5 miles from the sea side, there was another strong breastwork with 2 very great murderers to scoure the lane, where the enemy likewise appeared not; breif their strength was such that if the enemy had behaved himself manfully he mought have worsted us. It was Friday the 11th of May when the army marched into the town, about 2 in the afternoon. In the afternoon of Saturday the 12th a Spaniard with a white flag coming to our outguards, desiring a treaty was taken to the General. A treaty was agreed on, and 3 commissioned by their Governor, who was carried out of town in a hammock for the pox; meanwhile the enemy sent us 300 head of lean cattle, on purpose to make the least of the country.

On Tuesday the 15th it was agreed that the Spaniards should come out of the woods in a week where they would then lay down their arms, by the 16th of June to be transported to Nuova Spania [and] have each man take 2 suits of clothes, 4 shifts, and leave all their goods and negros with us, which may be about 3 or 4,000. The day before their time was to expire, they sent a letter (notwithstanding their 3 hostages whereof their poxy Governor was one) in to our Commissioners, [complaining of] the severity of the articles, to which if they complied, they were utterly ruined, and desired rather to expose their lives to the hazzard of war than to condescend to such terms. We endeavored to hold them to such terms as they gave us at Providence Island; our Commissioners were Major General Fortescue, Col. Holdhip, and Col. Doylie [ed.—Doylie: reference to Edward D'Oyley later appointed Governor of the island].

Upon this letter of the enemies our General, by advice of one of the Spanish Commissioners (who spoke against the treachery of the revolted Spaniards in the bushes, declaring them rebels if they did not submit not to the Articles), sent Col. Buller with 2,100 by sea and land to fall on the enemy near a river 7 leagues to leeward our town, [~24 miles likely towards the interior mountains] but the enemy was dispersed, and only a party of about 300 faced our party for a while, being most horse, and so went their ways never endeavouring to engage but to fly from us, having secured most of their best goods, their ordinary lumber, as beds, bedsteds, tables, and some chairs, lying scattered 3 or 4 miles to and again in the country. As for the town, which they call St. Jago of the Plain, there was found very little household stuff, and none but bedsteds, tables, and old chairs, except about 10,000 hides lying in the houses on the floors for their slaves etc. to lie on, which were brought into a church, ready to be sent to New England, for bisket, meat, and pease.

Friday, the last of May, Col. Buller returned with all his men in very good order and health, being only able to drive away the enemy, who of late had driven away the cattle from the savannahs near us, and so to discover the country, bringing no material plunder with them save some beds and tobacco. Upon consultation at his arrival, and considering that the only way to starve the enemy was to keep him from his Cassava bread, it was concluded that the next day a party of a 1,000 men should disperse and settle at several plantations, where the others should follow in due time, to inhabit the country, which will be divided among the regiments, and every man to have his proportion of goods from the province thereof, they managing it themselves. And for the going forward a committee is appointed for the benefit of the country. So far our voyage and design by land. By sea we keep upon this coast, to cruise and lie in wait for the enemies' ships, 12 friggats of good force, which are now ready to sail, and must attend this service till another squadron be sent to relieve them.

As for the country it is much like that of Hispaniola, in no way inferior, it has bigger plains, more and better water, most pleasant and healthful to the utmost, we have a land wind and a sea wind as at Hispaniola. The commodities of this country are sugar, Spanish tobacco, cotton, chocolate, hides, several sorts of wood as Lignum vitae, Brazil, or such sorts. Indigo will grow, so also wine and oile. The King of Spain to advance those 2 commodities having prohibited the growth thereof as the Spaniard tells us. Barley we have found and peas, so that we hope to brew beer and ale in time.

It is not so hot as Italy by day, and cooler by night and mornings. The days differ a little in length, at 7 of the clock it grows dark, and it is light at 5 in the morning. There are no other cities nor towns, but this on the island, and here we have above 1,000 houses; the streets not regular only some, many of the houses of good brick and timber covered with tile made heer, other houses of clay and reeds, which do reasonable well. We found only 2 small ships in the harbor, one was sunken, the other had chocolate, with wood tables and bedsteds ready made, and other goods. We have innumerable many wild and tame cattle that, feed by thousands on the savannahs, hogs, and horses also. The horse much better and larger than those of Hispaniola, so that better horse are [not] to be seen in England. Victuals here is therefore reasonable. We have butchers here that kill for the army, and we have sufficient thereof, and bread of Cassava with biscuit. The 3 rainy winter months are August, September, and October, after which the horse and cattle are very fat, and now at the worst some of them fat enough. We have now 2 of our ammunition and provision ships come to us, and the rest are at Barbados expected hourly: when we shall be so well provided of all things, that when we shall be satisfied, as we shall be suddenly, at the entringe in by the point and other places by sea, and at the landing, and at the town, we hope by God's gracious assistance to keep our station, in spite of the enemy who is round about us from the main and the Islands. Whereof I trust he shall be made sensible suddenly, and that we are in respect of our good harbor and situation. Better than if we had taken Hispaniola, as now our council and officers plainly see and acknowledge, so that it is to be questioned whether any place in the world would have advantaged our nation more than this. We have here a mine of copper, silver, if not one of gold, as the General has been informed by the Spaniards. We take horse and dragoones for each regiment, the enemy being about 4,000, whereof 600 Spaniards, and not 200 firearms. We have but 7 sugar mills yet found. Pray excuse the disorderly account I give you of this country, because of the haste I am in, and the care I take to settle. Mr. Wadeson our chief treasurer, goes with the hides to New England. Meanwhile I officiate as occasion is, but little will my business be I fear me, for the civil officers will have their pay in commodities of this country, unless our flax in these parts bring in money, whereof we despair not: by my next I shall tell you more of this country and conveniences thereof. St. Jago on Jamaica, 1 June 1655.

II

St. Jago on Jamaica, June 15, 1655 -- Our affairs here are much unsettled; the General and Col. Buller are following home to give account of matters, and to press for recruits, then have promised to return.

The enemy lie still in the mountains, expecting us to desert this country, but the rains now at hand will sweep them down amongst us or destroy them. We have taken 20 or 21 of them, among other a rich fat woman, the richest of the country; they annoy us not, but we have what cattle we please for driving in. The land is divided among the regiments, for money we have none, nor are we likely unless some prizes drop into our mouths at sea, whereof 3 or 4 are sunk and taken before St. Domingo, having left a frigate there.

III

June 16 . -- The General's and Colonel Buller's return to England is to vindicate the army from some aspersions, and doubts cast upon it by some great ones, and there will likely be a great debate about it in England, as also to hasten supplies of men and necessaries for such an undertaking, these return again within a year, or at least have engaged their honors for it to this council.

IV

July 15, 1655 -- Our General Venables with Colonel Buller are now taking their passage for England, full sore against the desire of almost every man, by what I understand, see that our troubles and discontents are added to those former confusions and wants of meat and drink wherein we lay involved, nevertheless we trust God will deliver us out of them in due time, who are somewhat comforted at the news of our last letters by the Charitie, dated in March last, whereby 14 sail, of victualls most, and some men of war, are upon their way towards us, the Protector withall promising us very fair. Meanwhile sickness hath destroyed a considerable part of our army, and about 1000 we have still remaining sick of the flux and fevers, (the usual diseases,) which have carried away almost all my best friends, as the Secretaries &c. but blessed be God who hath sent me health in the midst of sickness, and life when so many lie dead, I find my constitution still excellently agreeing with hot country. Nevertheless what through want of victualls onboard and ashore, together with the much sweating which this country is subject to, I am brought to that pass that I need not Dr Amie to keep me from pinguifying, being already fallen away 4 fingers about the waste, so that by this I like my voyage the better, though I have also learned patience thereby, and other particulars, which I think I could not have

45

learned at home; however this I can say, and I think there is not 20 of us can truly do the like, that I do not repent of my coming on this voyage. About 6 days since there came into us voluntarily 50 of the enemies, great and small, which we suppose the rain which already falls daily on the mountains hath caused, those parts, as we are told, being scarce habitable then: so that in all we have about 70 of the enemy among us, who have equal freedom and victuals with us as yet till the others are reduced, which we doubt not will be shortly; in the meantime they now oppresse us not, having not killed any of ours these 3 weeks, though before they dispatched about 100 of our stragglers unarmed; neither do we fear the enemy from the main, he having no shipping, nor we think force of men sufficient to oppose us. Our General goes home so very sick that we greatly fear he will not recover it, and Major General Fortescue, who is to be then the Commander in Chief, is also at present very ill. God grant these rainy months may beget some good alteration in point of health amongst us. Part of our General's business at home is to solicit that the army pay be otherwise than what we now have, and that we are not bound to take land in payment, as hitherto they have thought to invest each regiment with such a province or such partidos of land, which now they are cultivating, planting tobacco, Cassava bread etc, for sustenance and trade. This nonpayment nor hopes of any, makes so many Captains and others desire to go home, and to quit their interest, rather than be so badly paid as they count it.

V

Jamaica the 5 of November 1655

The 11 ships lately arrived to this place with &c. 1 poor men [*ed. note: likely referring to 1,800 men under Colonel Humphries*]. I pity them at the heart, all their imaginary mountains of gold are turned into dross, and their reason and affections are ready to bid them sail home again already. For my own part greater disappointments I never met with, having had no provisions in 10 weeks last past, nor above 3 biscuits this 14 weeks, so that all I can rape and scrape in ready money goes to housekeeping, and the shifts I make are not to be written here. We have lost half our army from our first landing on Hispaniola, when we were 8,000, besides 1,000 or more seamen in arms. Never did my eyes see such a sickly time, nor so many funerals, and graves all the town, over that it is a very Golgotha. We have a savannah or plane near us where some of the soldiers are buried so shallow that the Spanish dogs, which lurk about the town, scrape them up and eat them. As for English dogs they are most eaten by our soldiers; not one walks the streets that is not shot at, unless well befriended or respected. We have not only eaten all the cattle within near 12 miles of the place, but now also almost all the horse, asses, mules flesh near us, so that I shall hold little Eastcheap in more esteem than the whole Indies if this trade last, and I can give nor learn no reason that it should not bare continue so; besides this we expect no pay here, nor hardly at home now, but perhaps some ragged land at the best, and that but by the by spoken of, for us general officers not a word mentioned. I could dwell long upon this subject, and could tell you that still half our army lies sick and helpless, nor had we victuals for them before this fleet, nor expect ought now save some bread, and brandy, and oatmeal, and if that with phisick will not keep them alive, we have no other remedy but death for them. For my own part in 25 years have not I endured so much sickness as here with the bloody flux, rhume, ague, fever, so that I desire earnestly to go for England in March next, if permitted, for I am fallen away 5 inches about.

Amongst the dead persons your brother J. M. is one, who died of the dropsie, consumption, and other complicated diseases, the 22 of August 1655 last &c. we lately with 120 men and 12 frigotts took the towne of St. Martha on the Terra firma, where were 2 castles containing 32 peice of ordnance, out of which we beat the enemy by our ordnance, upon which the towns-men flying, our men presently landed and took the place with all therein, after an hour and a half skirmish, and 8 men lost on our part. The town and country, which we enjoyed 14 days, was far before this. They report 3/4 of the plunder went to the State, being all sold publicly, at which the soldiers grudge exceedingly, and I wish it spoil not the whole design; neither have we the liberty to transport those hides whereof we kill the beasts, whereby our men are wont to throw away the hides that they stink up and down the town. Our men demanded 2,0000 R. of 8 to ransom the place, which the enemy promised to give, but coming not at his time we fired the place, Churches and all.

—Source: *The Narrative of General Venables, a collection of letters and reports from the expedition, edited by historian C.H. Firth for the Royal Historical Society in 1900.*

1656

Cromwell Urges Settlers to Colonize Jamaica

Following England's capture of Jamaica in 1655, Oliver Cromwell sought to secure the island by encouraging English settlers from the American colonies and other Caribbean islands to relocate there. In particular, he petitioned inhabitants of New England in North America and smaller English-controlled islands such as Nevis to settle in Jamaica and strengthen England's foothold in the region.

The Migration from Nevis

One of the most notable responses came from Luke Stokes, a twice-serving English governor of Nevis. He led a migration of about 1,600 settlers—including his family—to Jamaica, establishing a settlement in Port Morant, an area in present-day St. Thomas. This marked the first major wave of English colonization on the island.

A Harsh Beginning: Disease and Death

The choice of Port Morant for the first settlement seemed promising at first. Located at the base of the Blue Mountains, it was one of the island's most fertile regions. Heavy rainfall fed numerous rivers, washing rich volcanic soil down from the mountains to create a fertile delta, ideal for agriculture. However, the same wet, low-lying conditions made it a breeding ground for mosquitoes carrying deadly diseases such as malaria and yellow fever.

Within a year of arrival, Luke Stokes, his wife, and nearly two-thirds of the settlers had died from disease. The few survivors abandoned the area, seeking higher, drier ground for safety. Some eventually settled inland, where the ruins of Stokes Hall Great House stand today.

Slow Development Until the Restoration

Despite Cromwell's efforts, Jamaica's development remained slow. The colony lacked a stable economy, and Spanish resistance in the mountainous interior—led by Maroon fighters and guerrilla forces—made it difficult for English settlers to establish full control.

However, this changed after the Restoration of King Charles II in 1660. As part of sweeping reforms:

- "The Point" was renamed Port Royal.
- Fort Cromwell was renamed Fort Charles.
- Privateering and buccaneering were encouraged to defend the island and harass Spanish ships.

By the 1670s, Port Royal had grown into one of the richest and most notorious towns in the New World, becoming a hub of piracy, commerce, and conflict between European powers—even after Spain formally ceded Jamaica to England under the Treaty of Madrid in 1670.

1657

The Spanish Gains a Foothold— Privateers Occupy Port Royal

The English conquest of Jamaica in 1655 did not bring immediate control of the island. For the next two years, England's grasp remained fragile—challenged not only by the terrain and disease, but by determined Spanish resistance, reinforced by a powerful and often-overlooked ally: the Maroons.

The Maroon Alliance

These Maroons were communities of formerly enslaved Africans who had escaped Spanish plantations, retreating into the mountainous interior long before the English invasion. There, they built independent settlements, honed their survival skills, and became masters of guerrilla warfare. Fiercely protective of their freedom and knowledge of the terrain, the Maroons became a critical force in the struggle for Jamaica's future.

The Spanish, recognizing their own diminishing foothold, offered the Maroons freedom, autonomy, and alliance in exchange for military support. For the Maroons, the English represented a new and growing threat to their independence. It was a calculated partnership. Maroon fighters ambushed English patrols, relayed intelligence to Spanish commanders, and harassed supply lines—making British consolidation of power slow and uncertain.

Ysassi's Offensive

Early in 1657, Don Cristóbal de Ysassi, the last Spanish governor of Jamaica, launched a new offensive to retake the island. He landed at Los Chorreros, near present-day Ocho Rios, with a force of Spanish soldiers and Maroon allies. But the English, now under the leadership of Colonel Edward D'Oyley, mounted a swift and effective defense, driving Ysassi and his forces to their ships and forcing a retreat to Cuba. It was a hard-won victory for the English—but far from the end of the struggle.

Strategic Importance of Cagway

Realizing that the capital and southern coast remained vulnerable to Spanish attacks, D'Oyley had taken decisive action. He saw promise in Cagway, a narrow sand spit guarding the entrance to Kingston Harbour—now known as Port Royal. Its deep waters and strategic location made it ideal for both defense and trade. But more than building fortifications, D'Oyley made a bold gamble—he invited privateers to make Cagway their home base.

The Rise of Port Royal

These were not ordinary settlers. They were privateers—state-sanctioned pirates, armed with letters of marque authorizing them to plunder Spanish ships. D'Oyley's move was both pragmatic and risky: by anchoring these freebooters at Cagway, he strengthened Jamaica's defenses without relying on overstretched English forces. Their presence would disrupt Spanish supply lines, discourage invasions, and bring economic activity to a struggling colony. It was a gamble that would ultimately turn Cagway into Port Royal, a name that would become synonymous with piracy, wealth, and excess.

Ysassi's Return and Rio Nuevo

But even as D'Oyley prepared the south, Ysassi had not given up.

Later in 1657, Ysassi returned to the island—this time with thirty companies of foot soldiers and a clearer plan. He sailed again from Cuba and landed not far from his previous defeat, further east along the coast at Rio Nuevo. There, the Spanish succeeded in establishing a fortified position—marking their strongest foothold in Jamaica since 1655.

A Colony at the Brink

For the English, this was a sobering development. Rio Nuevo offered the Spanish a staging ground for continued resistance, a potential rendezvous point for reinforcements from Cuba, and a secure base from which to coordinate with Maroon allies. The establishment of this outpost underscored just how tenuous English control remained.

Legacy of 1657

The events of 1657 tell the story of a colony still in flux. D'Oyley's decision to fortify Cagway and court privateers laid the groundwork for the rise of Port Royal and England's long-term naval dominance in the Caribbean. But the Spanish foothold at Rio Nuevo, strengthened by Maroon alliances, reminded all that the struggle for Jamaica was far from over.

The island was still contested—its future uncertain, its people divided, and its terrain a battleground of empire and resistance.

Juan de Bolas: The Maroon Who Became a British Colonel

In the years following the English conquest of Jamaica in 1655, the island's fate hung in the balance. Although the English had officially taken control, the occupying population consisted mostly of weary soldiers, sailors, and a few civilian camp followers. Disease, poor nutrition, and hostile terrain took a heavy toll. Pockets of Spanish resistance—bolstered by Maroons—posed a constant threat. The English faced persistent guerrilla warfare, and without firm control of the island's interior, colonization stalled. Spanish forces, supported by their Maroon allies, launched repeated raids on English positions, keeping Britain's grip on Jamaica fragile and uncertain.

The exact year and circumstances remain uncertain, but sometime during the period leading up to—and possibly after—the final Battle of Rio Nuevo in 1658, a pivotal shift occurred. Juan de Bolas, a prominent Maroon leader who had previously fought alongside the Spanish, defected to the English.

De Bolas's defection marked a turning point. The Maroons were skilled guerrilla fighters with an intimate knowledge of the island's rugged interior—it was their backyard. His decision to switch sides not only fractured the Maroon alliance but gave the English a powerful new advantage: a commander and his followers who were familiar with both the terrain and the guerrilla tactics used by the Maroons.

Though the full details of his agreement with the English are not well documented, it is believed that in exchange for his support, de Bolas and his followers were granted land, formal recognition, and military rank. He was appointed "Colonel of the Black Militia" by the English, making him the first man of

African descent in Jamaica to be granted official power under British rule. His forces assisted in rooting out remaining Spanish holdouts and suppressing further opposition, helping the English secure permanent control of the island.

De Bolas's legacy remains controversial. He was later assassinated—likely by Maroons still loyal to the Spanish cause —and over time, his story faded from national memory. Yet his actions and those of his followers, however divisive, played an important role in shaping the outcome of Jamaica's early colonial history.

Today, in the town of Lluidas Vale, near the region now known as the Juan de Bolas Mountains, a plaque commemorates his contribution. It reads:

> *Juan de Bolas lived and hunted on the mountain range you are facing. He was the 17th century warrior and political thinker, and also, at first, a resistance leader against the English invaders of 1655. But, in a stunning reversal, he helped change the course of our history from a Spanish-speaking people to English Jamaica. Juan de Bolas (his African name was Lubolo) saw that the former Spanish masters, who were losing to the English, had secured for themselves the ability to flee to Cuba. This would leave the blacks in the lurch. So he sensibly put the survival of his people first. He made a treaty with the English. He was made a Colonel by the English and he helped to secure their victory. He was assassinated by others of the mountain guerillas who favoured the Spanish cause.*
> *—Source: Commemorative Plaque, Lluidas Vale, Jamaica*

Though never formally recognized as a National Hero like Nanny or Sam Sharpe, Juan de Bolas was a defining figure in Jamaica's earliest struggles. His controversial choice played a part in changing the island's trajectory—and helped shape the Jamaica we know today.

1658

The Final Battle of Rio Nuevo

For two years, from 1655 to 1657, Don Cristóbal de Ysassi remained on the island, coordinating raids and guerrilla attacks with the support of Maroon allies, who had been promised freedom and autonomy in exchange for their military assistance. Their resistance from mountain hideouts made English consolidation of power slow and uncertain. It was only after his defeat at Los Chorreros in 1657 that Ysassi was forced to retreat to Cuba—though he would soon return.

The Foothold at Rio Nuevo

After a series of failed campaigns, Ysassi finally succeeded in 1658 in establishing a fortified position on the island's north coast at Rio Nuevo, in the parish of St. Mary. It was the strongest foothold the Spanish had secured since their initial expulsion. From this base, Ysassi hoped to launch a renewed offensive, reinforced by potential support from Cuba and continued cooperation with the Maroons, who remained committed to resisting English rule.

The Battle of Rio Nuevo

Between June 25 and 27, 1658, Colonel Edward D'Oyley, now the de facto English military leader in Jamaica, led a force of 750 soldiers in a decisive campaign to dislodge the Spanish from their fortified position. The confrontation—the Battle of Rio Nuevo—became the largest and bloodiest European military engagement ever fought on Jamaican soil.

Despite their defenses, the Spanish troops were outmaneuvered and overwhelmed. English firepower, superior discipline, and strategic advantage carried the day. Ysassi was forced to abandon the position and flee once again to Cuba. With this final defeat, the Spanish lost their last major stronghold and abandoned any serious efforts to retake Jamaica.

The Maroon Legacy

In a desperate final move, the Spanish had freed and armed their enslaved laborers, encouraging them to continue resisting the English. These newly freed fighters, along with earlier escapees from Spanish plantations, formed autonomous communities that would later be known collectively as the Maroons. Their deep knowledge of the terrain, tactical skill, and fierce commitment to freedom made them a lasting force in Jamaican resistance for over a century. Whether this was the moment Juan de Bolas changed allegiance—or if he had already joined the English ranks—remains a mystery.

A Nation Taking Shape

Following the victory at Rio Nuevo, Edward D'Oyley was confirmed as Jamaica's first official English governor, marking a shift from precarious occupation to formal governance. However, while military victory had been secured, Spain would not formally recognize England's possession of Jamaica until the Treaty of Madrid in 1670.

The Rio Nuevo Memorial

In recognition of the battle's significance, the Jamaican government declared the Rio Nuevo battle site a National Heritage Site in 1999. The land was donated by descendants of the Beckford family, prominent colonial-era plantation owners.

A memorial plaque at the site reads:

1658—The Death of Cromwell Ripples Across the Empire

In the same year that Jamaica's future was being contested in battle at Rio Nuevo, a seismic political shift occurred in England. On September 3, 1658, Oliver Cromwell, the Lord Protector of the English Commonwealth, died after years of illness. His death created a sudden power vacuum at the heart of the English government, triggering instability across the empire.

Cromwell had been the architect of England's short-lived republic and a key figure in the decision to invade and occupy Jamaica in 1655. His passing cast uncertainty over the island's military-backed colonial administration. In the immediate aftermath, his son, Richard Cromwell, inherited the title of Lord Protector—but lacked both the political acumen and military support that had sustained his father's rule.

Back in Jamaica, the death of Cromwell meant a growing lack of direction from London. For Edward D'Oyley and the English settlers, this reinforced the need for self-reliance. With Spain still threatening from the north and the colony in a fragile state of transition, local leaders had little choice but to continue asserting English control without clear guidance from the mainland.

While Cromwell's death took place across the ocean in England, it triggered the unraveling of the republic he had built—setting in motion the events that would lead to the restoration of the monarchy and reshape colonial rule in places like Jamaica.

1660

The Restoration of the English Monarchy and the Rise of Colonial Jamaica

King Charles I was executed in 1649, leading to the abolition of the English monarchy and the establishment of a Puritan republic under Oliver Cromwell. For 11 years, England remained a republic, with Cromwell ruling as Lord Protector.

Following Cromwell's death in 1658, his son Richard Cromwell briefly succeeded him but lacked his father's political skill and military support. Facing growing opposition, Richard was forced to resign in 1660, leading to the Restoration of the Monarchy.

That same year, Charles II, son of the executed king, who had lived in exile in Europe, was restored to the throne. In an act of retribution for his father's death, Charles II ordered a posthumous execution.

In 1661, on the 12th anniversary of King Charles I's execution, Cromwell's body was exhumed from Westminster Abbey along with the bodies of John Bradshaw (the judge who presided over

Charles I's trial) and Henry Ireton (Cromwell's son-in-law and a military leader). The three bodies were hanged in chains, beheaded after a mock execution, and their heads were placed on spikes above Westminster Hall. Cromwell's head remained on display for approximately 20 years as a public warning against rebellion.

Edward Doyley Appointed Governor and Establishment of a Governing Body

Edward Doyley emerged as the de facto leader of the struggling colony after the English conquest of Jamaica in 1655. He was first appointed as commander-in-chief of English forces in Jamaica, leading the island's defense against Spanish attempts to reclaim it. From 1655 to 1660, he governed under the title of Military Governor, overseeing both the military and administrative affairs of the island during its tumultuous early years under English rule.

Following the Restoration of the Monarchy in May 1660, King Charles II formally recognized Doyley as the first official Governor of Jamaica, transitioning the island from military rule to structured civil governance. Though some sources suggest that his official commission was finalized in 1661, his appointment as Governor effectively took place in 1660, marking the beginning of Jamaica's English colonial governance.

Doyley's tenure as governor was marked by efforts to stabilize English rule, strengthen the colony's defenses, and foster economic development. However, his position in office was short-lived—he was later replaced by Lord Windsor, who arrived with royal authority to implement England's long-term plans for Jamaica.

The following excerpt is taken from The History of Jamaica, Vol 1, by Edward Long, 1774. He was an English born historian, plantation owner and Jamaican jurist. His family had owned property in Jamaica since the early days of colonization.

After the conquest of Jamaica, part of the army was left for the security of the island, and the protection of those who should be induced to settle and plant there, martial law became the rule of their government, and was continued until the Restoration of King Charles II.

His majesty, bending his thoughts and councils to promote the prosperity of this colony, soon resolved, that the army should be disbanded, and that a civil government should be erected, under such known customs and laws as would render the island agreeable to the inhabitants, and beneficial to his kingdom.

Accordingly, colonel Edward D'Oyley, by his majesty's commission under the great seal of England, dated the 8th of February, 1660, was appointed governor of the island; and was directed to proceed forthwith to the election of a council, to consist of twelve persons, whereof the secretary of the island was to be one, and the rest to be fairly and indifferently chosen, by as many of the army, planters, and inhabitants, as by his best contrivance might be admitted; and, with their consent, the governor was empowered to act according to such just and reasonable customs and constitutions as were held and settled in his majesty's other colonies, or according to such other as, upon mature deliberation, should be held necessary for the good government and security of the island, "provided they were not repugnant to the laws of England."

In obedience to this commission, a council was elected by the colonists, in the nature of their representatives; several municipal laws were enacted; civil officers were constituted; and provision made, by a revenue act, to support the charge of government, which was then computed at 164 ol. per annum. But, the Spaniards remained a continued threat, the army was still kept on foot. This prevented the increase of the colony, and restrained the industry of the inhabitants. The planting business, and breeding of cattle, during this governor's administration received very little attention.

—*Source: The History of Jamaica, Vol 1, by Edward Long, 1774.*

The Rise of the Royal African Company and the Expansion of the Slave Trade

Charles II granted a royal charter to the Company of Royal Adventurers Trading to Africa, led by his younger brother, James, Duke of York (later King James II). The company was granted a monopoly over English trade along the West African coast, including commodities like gold, silver—and enslaved Africans.

Though the company collapsed in 1667 due to financial losses during the Second Anglo-Dutch War, it was revived and rechartered in 1672 as the Royal African Company. This company played a pivotal role in the transatlantic slave trade, transporting tens of thousands of enslaved Africans to the Caribbean and the Americas. Jamaica, now firmly under English control, became one of its primary markets, further entrenching plantation slavery as the foundation of its colonial economy.

1661

A New Governor and Expanded Rights for Settlers

After years of unstable governance under military rule, King Charles II sought to establish a more structured and effective colonial administration in Jamaica. The island had remained in a precarious state since the English conquest in 1655, with limited civilian leadership and ongoing resistance from Spanish forces and the Maroons. To address these challenges, on December 16, 1661, the King appointed Lord Windsor as Governor of Jamaica, replacing Edward Doyley, who had led the colony under military rule.

Lord Windsor's Appointment and Powers

Lord Windsor was granted broad and unprecedented powers, marking the first major step toward permanent English rule. Under his new commission, he was empowered to:

- Appoint a council to advise on colonial affairs.
- Call assemblies, giving settlers a voice in governance.
- Levy taxes in cases of emergency.
- Enact new laws, which could be enforced for two years without requiring the King's immediate approval.

Additionally, Lord Windsor formally disbanded the army and established a militia, creating a permanent defense force to protect the colony. This transition reflected England's long-term commitment to developing Jamaica as a self-sustaining colony rather than just a military outpost.

Royal Decree: Expanding Rights for Settlers

Recognizing the need to attract settlers and secure their loyalty, King Charles II issued a decree granting new rights and privileges to Jamaica's English inhabitants.

- Children of English-born settlers who were born in Jamaica were officially declared free denizens of England, with the same rights and privileges as any subject born in England.
- Other settlers—including those who had not been born in England—were granted additional privileges and

economic concessions to encourage immigration, land cultivation, and trade.

These measures were intended to motivate settlers to invest in the colony's future, help build an effective government, and entice new migrants from other English territories, particularly from Barbados and Nevis.

The Turning Point in Colonial Development

Lord Windsor's tenure, though brief, laid the foundation for Jamaica's transition into a stable and prosperous English colony. His appointment marked a shift from ad-hoc military rule to structured governance, setting the stage for Jamaica's transformation into a key economic and strategic hub in the West Indies.

By offering legal protections, property rights, and self-governance, England ensured that settlers had a vested interest in developing Jamaica's economy—particularly through plantation agriculture, trade, and piracy, which would soon define the island's future.

1663

The First General Elections in Jamaica

In December 1663, eight years after Jamaica became a British colony, the island held its first General Election, marking the establishment of formal colonial governance under English rule.

This event laid the foundation for the island's first elected legislative body, which would play a crucial role in shaping Jamaica's laws, taxation policies, and overall governance.

At the time of the election, Jamaica's total population was recorded at 4,205(*), consisting primarily of English settlers, indentured servants, a growing number of enslaved Africans, and a few freed blacks. However, only about 300 men were eligible to vote, as strict property and racial qualifications excluded most of the population from participating in the electoral process.

Voting Rights and Eligibility

The right to vote was highly restricted, reflecting the class-based and racialized nature of early English colonial politics. To be eligible, a voter had to meet the following criteria:

- Be a free white male
- Be at least 21 years old
- Own freehold property worth at least £10 OR pay a specified amount in taxes

Additionally, candidates seeking election to the Assembly faced even stricter financial requirements:

- They had to own freehold property worth at least £300 OR
- have a personal estate valued at no less than £3,000

This system ensured that political power remained concentrated in the hands of wealthy English landowners, while excluding small farmers, indentured servants, and the enslaved population from any form of representation.

A Colony in Transition

At the time of the election, Jamaica's economy was still in its early stages of development. While the town of Port Royal had begun to thrive as a commercial hub—largely due to privateering and trade—plantation agriculture had not yet fully taken hold beyond the town's immediate surroundings. The emerging legislative assembly would later be instrumental in passing laws that expanded the plantation economy and entrenched the institution of slavery as the primary labor system in Jamaica.

Legacy of the 1663 Elections

The establishment of an elected legislature in Jamaica reflected the broader English colonial model of governance, where local assemblies were granted limited powers while ultimate authority remained with the English Crown and appointed governors. However, it also marked the beginning of a long political struggle over power, representation, and autonomy—one that would continue into the 20th century as Jamaica moved toward full self-governance and independence.

(*) Editor's note: The population figure cited in the Commission's report has been updated to reflect official census data.
—Primary Source: History of the Electoral Commission of Jamaica - Prepared by the Electoral Commission of Jamaica September 2014

A Transformative Governor: Sir Thomas Modyford and the Expansion of Sugar & Privateering

In 1664, Sir Thomas Modyford arrived in Jamaica as its new Governor, bringing with him a vision for the island's transformation. A wealthy Barbadian planter and former Governor of Barbados, he was well-versed in colonial administration and had strong ties to King Charles II. His appointment came at a pivotal moment—Jamaica, newly taken from the Spanish nine years earlier, was still underdeveloped, poorly defended, and in dire need of an economic foundation.

The new Governor wasted no time. He understood that for England to truly secure Jamaica, it needed a thriving plantation economy, a larger population, and a formidable defense against Spanish retaliation. Within a few short years, he laid the foundation for what Jamaica would become—a prosperous sugar colony, a haven for privateers, and a stronghold of British power in the Caribbean.

Building a Sugar Empire

Modyford aggressively expanded sugar production, bringing in experienced planters from Barbados and offering land grants to fuel large-scale cultivation. Though sugar had already been introduced, his policies rapidly increased its importance, making it the dominant crop. He also secured a steady supply of enslaved Africans, dramatically increasing the labor force required for large-scale cultivation.

The results were swift—sugar quickly overtook other crops, marking the beginning of Jamaica's rise as one of the most valuable colonies in the British Empire. Under his leadership, estates grew, mills were built, and the island's economy became firmly tied to plantation slavery and the transatlantic trade.

Laying the Foundations of Government

Beyond agriculture, the governor pursued efforts to give Jamaica structure and legitimacy. Legal reforms were introduced to ensure landowners had secure property rights, and a more organized judicial system was established. To encourage settlement, he offered land and tax incentives, particularly to those migrating from Barbados and other Caribbean territories.

These initiatives provided stability and confidence, encouraging more English settlers to make Jamaica their home. The early years of his administration were crucial in transforming the island from a military conquest into a functioning English colony.

Port Royal: Privateering & Economic Growth

By the time of his arrival in 1664, English privateers were already operating out of Port Royal, thanks to a policy introduced by Edward Doyley in 1657. Rather than curtailing these activities, Modyford fully legitimized them, turning Port Royal into the official hub for privateering against Spain.

He expanded the issuance of letters of marque, granting even more English and French buccaneers the legal right to attack Spanish ships and settlements. Notorious privateers like Henry Morgan were welcomed, their raids actively encouraged.

The wealth pouring into Jamaica soon made Port Royal one of the busiest and most prosperous ports in the Americas. Through this strategic embrace of sanctioned piracy, the island became a major trading hub, where legitimate commerce and privateering thrived side by side.

Defending Jamaica from Spain

Aware that Spanish retaliation was inevitable, Modyford took deliberate steps to strengthen Jamaica's defenses. Port Royal and key coastal areas were fortified to ensure any attack would be met with resistance. The island's militia was expanded and trained, while privateers were effectively used as an unofficial navy to keep Spanish forces at bay.

This approach proved effective. Spain failed to retake Jamaica, and by the late 1660s, England's hold on the island had been solidified.

Securing Jamaica for England

Although recalled to England in 1671, the governor's policies had a lasting impact. His aggressive stance against Spain, combined with the economic strength he cultivated through sugar and privateering, ensured the island would remain in British hands. The groundwork he laid contributed to the Treaty of Madrid (1670), in which Spain formally ceded Jamaica and agreed to cease hostilities.

A Controversial End

Despite his success, Modyford's unapologetic embrace of privateering led to his downfall. In 1671, with England seeking better diplomatic relations with Spain, he was recalled and imprisoned in the Tower of London. Yet, without formal charges, he was eventually released.

His legacy, however, was undeniable. Under his leadership, Jamaica had been firmly secured as a British stronghold. What had once been a neglected Spanish outpost had transformed into a vital colony, an emerging economic powerhouse, and one of the most infamous privateering hubs in the world.

1668

Port Royal Rises as a Hub for Piracy

By 1668, Port Royal had cemented its reputation as the most notorious privateering stronghold in the Caribbean. Under Governor Sir Thomas Modyford's leadership, Jamaica had become a haven for English privateers, who launched raids on Spain's American territories with tacit government support. Modyford understood that privateering not only weakened Spain's dominance but also fueled Jamaica's economy, bringing in wealth and trade.

Henry Morgan's Rise to Power

One of the most significant events of the year was Henry

Morgan's rise to leadership among the privateers. Edward Mansfield, a notorious English privateer and pirate, had commanded the Brethren of the Coast, a powerful confederation of English and French buccaneers. Operating from Port Royal, Jamaica, he played a key role in establishing the city as a major privateering hub under English rule. As Morgan's mentor, Mansfield passed down both tactical knowledge and influence, shaping Morgan's ascent.

When Mansfield died, Morgan was elected Admiral of the Brethren of the Coast, effectively assuming command of the privateering fleet operating out of Port Royal. His elevation marked a turning point in Jamaica's privateering history, as he would go on to lead some of the most daring raids against Spanish strongholds.

Morgan's Raid on Portobello

Seeking to cripple Spanish defenses and plunder their wealth, Morgan assembled a formidable force of English and French privateers, as well as a Dutch captain, for an audacious attack on Portobello, one of Spain's wealthiest ports in Panama. His fleet set sail from Port Royal, anchoring near the Panamanian coast under the cover of night. Under the shadows, the raiders navigated to a secluded landing point, then stealthily crossed the mountains, catching the town by surprise.

They quickly overran the first fort overlooking the settlement before storming the second, which protected the harbor. The Spanish defenders fought fiercely, but Morgan's men breached the fortifications and seized control. To avoid further destruction, Spanish officials eventually negotiated a ransom to spare the town's fortifications and its stockpiled gunpowder.

Morgan's fleet returned to Port Royal with immense riches, further fueling the town's prosperity. However, the victory came at a heavy cost—along with Spanish gold, the privateers unknowingly brought back disease. An outbreak of plague swept through Port Royal, claiming many lives, including Lady Modyford, the governor's wife.

Port Royal's Rise & The Expanding Influence of Privateering

Despite the plague, Port Royal continued to grow into the most prosperous and infamous city in the Caribbean. Privateers spent their fortunes in its taverns, merchants thrived on the influx of wealth, and the English government unofficially benefited from the plundered Spanish treasure. Morgan's success at Portobello only strengthened the privateering culture, reinforcing Port Royal's status as the pirate capital of the West Indies.

However, as English-Spanish relations evolved, the era of unrestricted privateering would not last forever. While Morgan's triumphs brought Jamaica wealth and notoriety, they also placed increasing diplomatic pressure on England to curb piracy —a tension that would come to a head in the years to follow.

—*Primary Source: Trapham, Thomas. The Present State of Jamaica, with the Life of the Great Columbus – pub 1683*

1670

The Treaty of Madrid: Spain Recognizes England's Control of Jamaica

The Treaty of Madrid, signed on July 18, 1670, formally ended hostilities between England and Spain in the Americas and marked a turning point in Jamaica's development. For the first time, Spain officially recognized England's sovereignty over Jamaica, putting an end to years of uncertainty that had discouraged settlement and investment.

With the Spanish threat diminished, Jamaica's economy began to grow more rapidly. New settlers arrived from England and other British colonies, encouraged by increased security and the island's expanding sugar industry. Trade between England and Spain also opened up, further stimulating economic activity.

However, the treaty also had a major impact on piracy. As part of the agreement, England pledged to suppress piracy in the Caribbean, while Spain agreed to grant English ships greater freedom of movement. Although privateering had played a crucial role in Jamaica's defense and economy, the treaty signaled the beginning of a shift—one that would eventually lead to the decline of state-sponsored piracy.

1671

Henry Morgan's Raid on Panama and His Arrest

In the years following his appointment as Admiral in 1668, Henry Morgan launched increasingly daring and lucrative raids on Spanish strongholds. Encouraged by his previous victories, he set his sights on Panama City, the wealthiest Spanish port on the Pacific coast. In late 1670, Morgan assembled a large force of buccaneers and embarked on one of the most ambitious raids of his career.

Morgan and his men crossed the Isthmus of Panama, enduring extreme hardships before launching a devastating attack on January 28, 1671. They overwhelmed the Spanish defenders, sacked the city, and looted its immense wealth. Amidst the chaos, a massive fire broke out, destroying much of Panama City.

It remains unclear whether Morgan knew of the treaty before the raid. Some historians speculate he may have deliberately ignored it, believing England would still tolerate privateering as long as it remained profitable. Regardless, the destruction of Panama City infuriated the Spanish crown and caused deep embarrassment for the English government, forcing them to take action against Morgan.

Upon his return to Jamaica, Morgan was arrested and sent to England, along with Governor Sir Thomas Modyford, who had authorized privateering commissions. However, Morgan's imprisonment was largely symbolic—he was never formally charged with any crime. By 1674, political tides had shifted once again, and Morgan was knighted by King Charles II and appointed Lieutenant Governor of Jamaica.

The Recall of Modyford and the Slow Decline of Piracy

Sir Thomas Modyford was recalled to England in 1671, largely due to his open support of privateering. While his policies had strengthened Jamaica's economy and defenses, his encouragement of raids against Spain had become a diplomatic liability. Unlike Morgan, however, Modyford did not return to Jamaica—he remained in England and was eventually released from house arrest. He spent the rest of his life as a respected planter in England.

The Treaty of Madrid set in motion the eventual decline of piracy in the Caribbean. With England and Spain officially at peace, public sentiment toward piracy began to shift. English authorities, particularly in London, grew less tolerant of privateering, especially as merchants and plantation owners sought more stable trade relations. However, piracy did not disappear immediately.

Despite the treaty's terms, English governors in Jamaica were reluctant to immediately suppress privateering. The English still relied on privateers as a defensive force against Spain, and Port Royal remained a stronghold for sanctioned raids. However, the official stance toward piracy gradually shifted, and by the 1680s, privateering began to decline, culminating in the end of the Golden Age of Piracy by the 1720s.

Transition from Piracy to Commerce

With Modyford recalled to England and Morgan under arrest, Jamaica's relationship with privateering entered a period of uncertainty. The Treaty of Madrid signaled a shift in England's priorities, reducing its reliance on buccaneers while focusing on long-term economic stability. Though piracy persisted, Jamaica's survival could no longer depend solely on raiding Spanish territories.

As Jamaica moved beyond its early years of conflict, attention shifted toward legitimate trade and economic expansion. While sugar was still in its infancy, the island's economy was already benefiting from a diverse range of valuable exports. Logwood, highly sought after in Europe's textile and dyeing industries, became Jamaica's first major export under British rule, driving economic growth and shaping the fortunes of towns like Black River.

At the same time, indigo and cacao emerged as lucrative crops.

Indigo, prized for its deep blue dye, was essential to the European textile industry, while cacao, used to make chocolate, remained a luxury commodity in high demand. However, Jamaica's early cacao industry suffered setbacks due to plant disease in the early 1670s, limiting its long-term success.

Despite these challenges, Jamaica's strategic location and expanding trade networks positioned it as a key supplier of raw materials. This period of economic diversification laid the foundation for the plantation-driven economy that would soon be dominated by sugar production and sustained by the transatlantic slave trade.

1671 - The Logwood Boom: Jamaica's First Major Export Under British Rule

By 1671, logwood had become Jamaica's first significant export crop under British rule. This tropical hardwood, which thrived in the island's coastal swamps, was highly sought after in Europe's booming textile industry. When cut and processed, logwood produced deep red, purple, and black dyes, making it one of the most valuable commodities of the era.

The demand for logwood was so intense that it became a focal point of international conflict, with British, Spanish, and French privateers all vying for control of the lucrative trade routes. Logwood extraction required little initial investment, making it an accessible venture for early British settlers. By 1680, logwood exports had grown to rival sugar in economic importance.

Black River: The Center of the Logwood Trade

As logwood exports surged, the town of Black River emerged as Jamaica's primary hub for the trade, with its deep natural harbor providing the perfect location for shipping vast quantities to England, Europe, and North America. Situated along the southwest coast near the Great Morass, a vast wetland teeming with logwood trees, Black River quickly became one of Jamaica's wealthiest settlements.

The influx of logwood wealth transformed Black River into a thriving commercial center, where British merchants and local traders controlled the island's most lucrative early export. By the early 18th century, it had developed:

- One of the busiest ports in Jamaica, handling massive logwood shipments.
- A prosperous merchant class, with British traders amassing great wealth.
- Early modern infrastructure, including paved streets and grand houses, making Black River one of Jamaica's first 'modern' towns.

However, by the late 19th century, the logwood industry declined as synthetic dyes emerged in Europe, eliminating the need for natural alternatives. As demand faded, Black River's economy had to shift, later becoming a hub for banana exports, shipping, and eventually tourism.

A Lasting Legacy

Though logwood is no longer a major export, its influence remains embedded in the story of Black River. Once a bustling hub of commerce, the town thrived on the wealth generated by the logwood trade. Strategically positioned on the south coast, Black River's harbor allowed ships to carry logwood from Jamaica's interior to eager markets overseas. Its port, one of the busiest on the island, served as a gateway for the valuable hardwood, destined for European dye markets. For decades, the town's prosperity was reflected in its fine Georgian and Victorian architecture, including Magdala House and Invercauld

Great House, built by the Leyden and Farquharson families during the 1880s and 1890s. These stately homes stand as reminders of the fortunes that logwood brought to Black River.

Even as the demand for logwood waned with the rise of synthetic dyes in the late 19th century, the wealth it generated had left its mark. The town's prominence lingered, and its affluence was evident in milestones like its distinction as the first town in Jamaica to introduce electricity in 1893, a reflection of its once-thriving economy. But the decline of the logwood trade, coupled with the growing dominance of sugar, gradually shifted the economic tide.

Today, Black River moves at a quieter pace. The once-thriving port remains, now serving local fishermen and small vessels rather than merchant fleets. The echoes of its logwood legacy endure in the weathered facades of historic buildings, standing as silent witnesses to an era when Black River played a central role in Jamaica's global trade. While the town's golden age has passed, its story is an important chapter in the island's history— a testament to the role Black River played in Jamaica's economic and cultural development.

1672

Henry Morgan Arrested & The Expansion of The Slave Trade

In April 1672, Henry Morgan was arrested upon his return to Jamaica and sent to England to face charges. Initially imprisoned, his fate took an unexpected turn as shifting political dynamics in England worked in his favor. By 1674, he was pardoned and knighted by King Charles II, who appointed him Lieutenant Governor of Jamaica. Morgan later retired as a wealthy and influential planter, cementing his legacy in the colony.

While Morgan's fate was being decided in England, another transformation was taking place—one that would fundamentally reshape Jamaica's economy and society: the formalization of the transatlantic slave trade.

The Royal African Company and the Expansion of the Slave Trade

In 1672, a new company was formed: the Royal African Company (RAC), receiving a royal charter that granted it a monopoly over the English slave trade. It was a rebranding of the Company of Royal Adventurers Trading to Africa, originally established in 1660 under the leadership of James, Duke of York (the king's brother). The original company had ambitious plans to dominate trade along the West African coast, particularly in gold, ivory, and enslaved Africans. However, it struggled with mounting debt and mismanagement, and by 1667, it had collapsed under financial strain.

To revive England's stake in the lucrative transatlantic slave trade, the Royal African Company was restructured and granted exclusive rights to trade in African captives. Unlike its predecessor, which had focused more broadly on commodities, the RAC introduced a systematic, large-scale model of human trafficking, ensuring a steady and efficient supply of enslaved laborers to British colonies.

Operating from fortified bases along the West African coast, including Cape Coast Castle and James Fort, the RAC shipped thousands of enslaved Africans across the Atlantic each year. Between 1680 and 1686, it transported an average of 5,000 enslaved Africans annually, branding them with the company's initials—"RAC"—before selling them in British colonies such as Jamaica, Barbados, and Virginia.

Jamaica Becomes a Major Slave Market

By the early 1670s, Jamaica had become one of the busiest slave markets in the Atlantic, supplying labor not only to British plantations but also fueling a thriving smuggling trade with Spanish America. The island's central location and growing demand for enslaved labor cemented its role as a crucial distribution hub in the Caribbean slave economy.

At the same time, Jamaica's economy expanded rapidly, driven by the production of sugar, indigo, logwood, and cacao. However, a plant disease devastated the cacao industry in 1670–1671, forcing planters to shift their focus toward sugar and logwood, two commodities that would soon dominate the island's economy.

As European demand for natural dyes surged, logwood remained a highly profitable export. Meanwhile, sugar production expanded at an even greater pace, eventually surpassing all other industries. This transformation solidified Jamaica's place as one of the British Empire's most valuable colonies and set the stage for its economic future.

With enslaved Africans arriving in increasing numbers, they soon outnumbered Europeans on the island by a ratio of 5 to 1— a demographic shift that would shape Jamaica's social and economic structure for centuries. The influx of wealth and trade also fueled political developments, as colonists sought greater control over the island's governance.

By the mid-1670s, Jamaican settlers formed a local legislature—an early step toward self-government. However, political power remained concentrated in the hands of wealthy plantation owners, ensuring that governance served the interests of the colony's elite rather than the broader population.

1692

The Port Royal Earthquake and the Founding of Kingston

By the late 17th century, Port Royal had become one of the busiest trading centers in the British West Indies, its bustling economy rivaling that of larger colonial cities like Boston. It was known throughout the New World for its immense wealth, extravagant lifestyle, and infamous reputation for vice and debauchery. Merchants, artisans, and tavern owners flocked to the town to serve the needs of privateers and pirates who poured their riches into the local economy. By 1692, the population exceeded 8,000, living in fine brick buildings, some rising up to four stories high, all packed into an area of approximately 50 acres. The city was widely known as "the richest and wickedest city in the New World."

The Earthquake

On June 7, 1692, a massive earthquake struck Port Royal, bringing devastation in minutes.

The Rector of Port Royal later recounted in two letters how, while enjoying a drink of wormwood wine with the acting Governor, John White, he suddenly felt the ground rolling beneath his feet. "Lord, Sir, what is that?" he asked. "It's an earthquake," his friend replied. Moments later, the church tower collapsed. As they fled for safety, the ground split open, swallowing people whole, while the sea surged in over the town's fortifications. The family the Rector had planned to dine with that day was among those lost to the quake and flood. "Had I been there," he wrote, "I would have been lost."

The earthquake caused roughly two-thirds of Port Royal—its entire western end—to sink into the Caribbean Sea. Thousands perished in minutes. In the days that followed, the devastation worsened: disease spread, the stench of the dead hung in the air, and survivors described dogs gnawing on corpses partially buried by the collapse. The event was one of the most catastrophic natural disasters in Caribbean history and served as a brutal turning point in Jamaica's colonial era.

In the wake of Port Royal's destruction, the colonial authorities acted swiftly to establish a new town across the harbor to resettle the survivors. Just two weeks after the earthquake, the government purchased 200 acres of land from Sir William Beeston, a prominent merchant and colonial official, for £1,000. At the time, Beeston was away from the island, so the transaction was handled through his lawyer. The land had originally been owned by Colonel Samuel Barry and was known as Colonel Barry's Hog Crawle, a name reflecting its former use as a hog-raising area.

Surveyor John Goffe was commissioned to design the layout for the new town. Opting for a practical and orderly design, he implemented a grid system of perpendicular streets and lanes, with boundaries stretching one mile inland from the harbor (Port Royal Street to North Street) and a half-mile across from

East Street to West Street. At the heart of the town, the intersecting King Street and Queen Street—each 66 feet wide—formed four quadrants around a central square. This square, intended as the town's focal point, was designated to house a Parade Ground, a church, and military barracks.

In recognition of the men associated with the land's transfer, the first two streets flanking the Parade were named Beeston Street and Barry Street—after Sir William Beeston and Colonel Samuel Barry, respectively.

Initially, temporary huts were built to house earthquake refugees, with the government offering plots of land on the condition that homes be constructed within three years. These early foundations soon gave rise to Kingston, a city that not only sheltered the survivors of Port Royal but grew to surpass its predecessor in both size and significance, becoming Jamaica's enduring commercial and political center.

EyeWitness Account of the 1692 Port Royal Earthquake

In the aftermath of the catastrophic earthquake that struck Port Royal, Jamaica, on June 7, 1692, Reverend Emmanuel Heath, an Anglican rector and eyewitness to the disaster, penned two harrowing letters that provide one of the most vivid and detailed accounts of the event. Written on June 22 and June 28, 1692, these letters capture both the physical destruction wrought by the earthquake and its profound impact on the lives of those who survived.

The following passage presents an eyewitness account of the devastating earthquake that struck Port Royal, Jamaica, on June 7, 1692, as published in The British Gazetteer in March 1756. The account is framed around two letters written by Reverend Emmanuel Heath, the Anglican rector of St. Paul's Church, in Port Royal in the immediate aftermath of the disaster.

To provide a more complete picture of the event and its widespread consequences, the Gazetteer augmented Reverend Heath's personal narrative with details from other contemporary sources, including reports transmitted to the Royal Society of London and observations on the ensuing sickness and weather patterns. This rewritten passage aims to capture the entirety of the Gazetteer's presentation, offering a vivid and accessible narrative for modern readers that blends Reverend Heath's eyewitness experiences with broader details of the catastrophe.

The following excerpt have been lightly edited for readability. Original language and spelling have been preserved where possible. Passages where the exact meaning is unclear have been left as written.

Reverend Emmanuel Heath: Eye Witness Account of 1692 Earthquake

As Published in The British Gazetteer, March 1756

The first letter dated June 22, 1692

Dear Friend,

I Doubt not but you will, both from Gazettes, and Letters hear of the great Calamity that hath befallen this Island by a terrible Earthquake, on the 7th instant, which hath thrown down almost all the Houses, Churches, Sugar-Works, Mills and Bridges, through the whole Country. It tore the Rocks and Mountains, destroyed some whole Plantations, and threw them into the Sea, Port-Royal had much the greatest share in this terrible Judgement of God. I will therefore be more particular in giving you an account of its proceedings in this Place, that you may know what my Danger, and how unexpected my Preservation.

On Wednesday the 7th of June I had been as Church reading Prayers, which I did every day since I was Rector of Port-Royal, to keep up some shew of Religion among a most ungodly debauched people; and was gone to a place hard by the Church, where the merchants use to meet, and where the President of the Council was, who acts now in Chief till we have a new Governor. This Gentleman came into my Company, and engaged me to take a Glass of Wormwood-wine with him as a whet before Dinner.

He being my very great friend, I stayed with him. Hereupon he lighted a Pipe of Tobacco, which he was pretty long of taking; and not being willing to leave him before it was out, this detained me from going to Dinner to one Captain Ruden's, where I was to dine, whose House, upon first Convulsion sunk first into the Earth, and then into the Sea, with his Wife and Family, and some who were come to dine with him. Had I been there, I had been lost. But to return to the President, and his Pipe of Tobacco. Before that was out, I found the ground rolling and moving under my feet, upon which I said, Lord, Sir, what is that? He replied very composedly, being a very grave Man, It's an Earthquake; be not afraid, it will soon be over. But it increased, and we heard the Church and Tower fall, upon which we ran to save our selves; I quickly lost him, and made towards Morgan's Fort, which being a wide place, I thought to be there securest from the falling Houses. But as I made toward it, I saw the Earth open and swallow up a Multitude of People, and the Sea mounting in upon us over the Fortifications.

I then laid aside all thoughts of escaping, and resolved to make toward my own Lodging, and there to meet Death in as good a posture as I could. From the Place where I was, I was forced to cross, and run through two or three very narrow Streets. The Houses and Walls fell on each side of me. Some Bricks came rolling over my shoes, but none hurt me. When I came to my Lodging, I found all things in the same order I left them, not a picture, of which there were several fair ones in my Chamber, being out of its place. I went to my Balcony to view the street in which our house stood, and saw never a house down there, nor the ground so much as crack'd.

The people seeing me, cried out to me to come and pray with them. When I came into the street every one laid hold my Cloaths, and embraced me, that with their Fear and Kindness I was almost stifled. I at last persuaded them to kneel down, and make a large Ring, which they did. I pray'd with them near an hour, when I was almost *spent with the heat of the sun and the exercise. They then brought me a Chair; the Earth working all the while with new motions, and tremblings, like the rollings of the Sea; insomuch that sometimes, when I was at Prayers. I could hardly keep myself upon my knees.*

By that time I had been half an hour longer with them, in setting before their Sins and heinous Provocations, and seriously exhorting them to Repentance, there came some Merchants of the Place, who desired me to go on board some ship in the Harbour and refresh myself, telling me that they had a Boat to carry me off. I found the Sea had entirely swallow'd up the Wharf, with all the goodly Brick houses upon it, most of them as fine as those in Chepside, and two entire streets beyond that. From the tops of some houses which lay levelled with the surface of the Water, I got first into a Canoe, and then into a Long Boat, which put me aboard a Ship called the Siam-Merchant. There I found the President safe, who was overjoyed to see me, and continued there that night, but could not sleep for the returns of the Earthquake, almost every hour, which made all the Guns in the Ship to jar and rattle.

The next day I went from Ship to Ship to visit those that were bruised, and dying; likewise to do the last Office at the sinking of several Corps that came floating from the Point. This, indeed has been my sorrowful employment ever since I came aboard this Ship with design to come for England; we having had nothing but shakings of the Earth, with Thunder and Lightning, and foul Weather ever since. Besides the people being so desperately wicked, it makes me afraid to stay in the place; for that every day this terrible Earthquake happen'd, as soon as night came on, a Company of lewd Rogues whom they call Privateers, fell to breaking open Warehouses, and Houses deserted, to rob and rifle their Neighbors, whilst the Earth trembled under them, and the Houses fell on some of them in the Act; and those audacious Whores that remain upon the Place, are as impudent and drunken as ever.

I Have been twice on shoar to pray with the bruised and dying People, and to christen Children, where I found too many drunk and swearing. I did not spare them, nor the Magistrates neither, who have suffer'd Wickedness to grow to so great a height. I have, I bless God, to the best of my skill and power, discharged my Duty in this place, which you will hear from most persons, who come from hence,

I have preached so seasonably to them, and so plain. In the last sermon I deliver'd in the Church; I set before them what would be the issue of their Impenitence and Wickedness, so clearly, that they have since acknowledged, it was more like a Prophecy than a Sermon: I had, I confess, an impulse upon me to do it; And many times I have preached in this Pulpit, things which I never premeditated at home, and could not methought, do otherwise.

The day when all this befel us was, was very clear, and afforded not the suspicion of the least evil; but in the space of three Minutes, about half an Hour after Eleven in the Morning, Port Royal, the fairest Town of all the English Plantations, the best Emporium and Mart of this part of the World, exceeding in its Riches, plentiful of all good Things, was shaken and shattered to pieces, and sunk into, and cover'd for the greatest Part, by the Sea, and will in a short time be wholly eaten up by it; for few of those houses which yet stand, are left whole, and every day we hear them fall, and the Sea daily encroaches upon it; We guess, that by the falling of the Houses, opening of the Earth, and the Inundation of the Waters, there are lost 1500 persons, and many of good note; of whom my good friend Attorney General Musgrove, is one, my Lord Secretary Reves is another. William Turner, Thomas Turner's Brother is lost. Mr. Swymer escaped, but his house-mate Mr. Watts, perished.

I came, I told you, on board this Ship in order to return home, but the People are so importunate with me to stay, that I know not what to say to them. I must undergo great hardship if I continue here, the Country being broke to pieces and dissected. I must now live in a Hutt, eat Yams, and Plantants for Bread, which I could never endure; drink Rum-punch and Water, which were never pleasing to me.

I have written to send a younger Person, who may better endure the Fatigue of it than I can: But if I should leave now, it will look very unnatural to leave them in their distress, and therefore whatever I suffer, I would not have such a blame lie at my door, so I am resolved to continue with them a year longer. They are going all in haste, to build a new Town near the Rock Linavea, [ed. possibly Kingston near Liguanea] the Guardian of this Island. The French from Pituguaveis, or Petitgeavias, in Hispaniola, did attack this Island on the North side; but were all defeated and destroyed, it being about the time of the Earthquake.

The Second Letter, dated June 28, 1692.

Ever since that fatal day, the most terrible that ever I saw in my life, I have lived on Board a Ship; for the shaking of the Earth return every now and then. Yesterday we had a very great one, but it seems less terrible on Ship-board than on Shore; yet I have ventur'd to Port Royal no less than three times since its desolation, among the shattered Houses to bury the Dead, pray with the Sick, and christen the Children. Sunday last I preached among them in a Tent, the Houses that remain being so shattered, I durst not venture to preach in them. The People are overjoy'd to see me among them, and wept bitterly when I preach'd. I hope by this terrible Judgement, God will make them reform their lives, for there was not a more ungodly People on the Face of the Earth.

It is a sad sight to see all this Harbour, one of the fairest and goodliest I ever saw, covered with the dead Bodies of People of all conditions, floating up and down without burial; for our great and famous Burial Place, called the Palisadoes was destroyed by the Earthquake; which dashing to pieces the Tombs, whereof there were Hundreds in that Place, Sea washed the Carcasses of those that were buried out of their Graves.

Multitudes of Rich Men are utterly ruin'd, whilst many, who were poor, by watching opportunities, and searching the wrecked and sunk Houses, (even almost while the Earthquake lasted, and terror was upon all the considerable People), have gotten great riches.

We have had Accounts from several Parts of the Island, of the Mischiefs done by the Earthquake. From St Anne's we hear of 1,000 acres of Woodland changed into the Sea and carrying with it whole Plantations. But no place suffered like Port Royal; where the streets (with Inhabitants) were swallowed up by the opening of the Earth, which then shutting upon them, squeezed the People to Death. And in that manner several were buried with their heads above Ground; only some Heads the Dogs have eaten; others are covered with Dust and Earth, by the people who yet remained in the Place, to avoid the Stench.

Thus I have told you a long and sad story, and God knows what worse may happen yet. The people tell me that they hear great Bellowings and Noises in the Mountains; which makes some very apprehensive of an Eruption of Fire; if so, it will, I fear, be more destructive than the Earthquake. I am afraid to stay, and yet I know not how in Point of Conscience, at such a juncture as this, to quit my Station.

[Additional Accounts Included in The British Gazetteer's Report]

Several accounts of this desolating Earthquake were likewise transmitted to the Royal Society at London, from several Persons then residing in Jamaica; the particulars of which are as follow:

The earth opened and swallowed up people, and they role in other Streets; some in the Middle of the Harbour, and yet were saved; tho' there were 2000 People loft, and 1000 Acres of Land sunk.

All the Houses were thrown down throughout the island. One Hopkins and his Plantation remov'd half a mile from the Place.

Of all Wells, from one Fathom to six or seven, the Water flew out of the Top with a vehement Motion.

While the Houses, on one Side of the Street were swallow'd up, on the other there were thrown in Heaps; and the Sand in the Street rose like waves in the Sea, lifting up every Body that stood on it, and immediately dropping down into Pits; and at the same Instant a Flood of Water breaking in, rolled them over and over; some catching hold of Beams, Rafters, &c.

Ships and Sloops in the Harbour were overset and loft; the Swan Figrate particularly, by the Motion of the Sea, and the sinking of the Wharf, was driven over the Tops of many Houses.

It was attended with a hollow rumbling Noise, like that of Thunder. In less than a Minute three Quarter of the Houses, and the Ground they stood on, with Inhabitants, were all sunk quite under Water; and the little Part left behind, was no better than Rubbish.

The shock was so violent, that it threw People down on their Knees, or their Faces, as they were running about for Shelter. The Ground heav'd and swell'd like the rolling Sea; and several Houses, still standing, were shuffled and mov'd several Yards out of their Places.

A whole Street is said to be twice as broad now as it was before; and in many Places the Earth would crack and open, and shut quick and fast. Of which Openings two or three hundred might be seen at a Time; in some whereof the People were swallow'd up; others, the closing Earth caught by the Middle, and pressed to Death; in others, the Heads only appear'd.

The larger Openings swallowed up Houses; and out of some would issue whole Rivers of Waters, spouted up a great height into the Air, and threatening a Deluge to that Part the Earthquake spared.

The Whole was attended with Stenches and offensive Smells, the Noise of the falling Mountains at a distance, &c. and the Sky in a Minute's Time, was turn'd dull and reddish, like a glowing oven.

Yet, as great a Sufferer as Port Royal was, more Houses were left standing therein, than the whole island beside.

Scare a Planting-house, or sugar-work, was left standing in all Jamaica. A great part of them were swallow'd up, Houses, People, Trees, and all at one Gape; in Lieu of which afterwards appear'd great Pools of Water, which when dried up, left nothing but Sand, without any Mark, that ever Tree, or Plant, had been thereon.

Above 12 miles from the Sea, the Earth gaped, and spouted out, with a prodigious Force, vast Quantities of Water into the Air, yet the greatest Violences were among the Mountains and Rocks; and it is a general Opinion, that the nearer the Mountains, the greater the Shake; and that the Cause thereof lay there.

Most of the Rivers were stopped up for 24 Hours, by the falling of the Mountains; till swelling up, they made themselves new Tracks and Channels; tearing up, in their Passage, Tree &c.

After the great Shake, those people who escaped, got onboard ships in the Harbour, where many continued above two Months: the Shakes being all that Time so violent, and coming so thick sometimes two or three in an Hour, accompanied with frightful Noises, like the ruffling Wind, or a hollow rumbling Thunder, with Brimstone Blasts, that they durst not come ashore.

The consequences of the earthquake was a general Sickness, from the noisome vapours belched forth, which swept away above 3000 Persons.

As soon as the violent Shake was over, the Minister desired all People to join with him in Prayer; and among them were several Jews, who kneel'd and answer'd as the rest did; nay, the Author was told, that they were heard to call upon Jesus Christ; a Thing says he, worth Observation!

The two great Mountains at the Entrance of 16 Mile-walk, fell, and meeting, stopt the River; so it was dry, from that place to the Ferry, for a whole Day; and vast Quantities of Filth were taken up, greatly to the Relief of the distressed and terrified Inhabitants.

At Yellows, a great Mountain split, and falling into the level land, cover'd several Settlements, and destroy'd 19 white People. Had the Shake happen'd in the Night, very few would have escaped.

But the Mortality which ensued the great Earthquake (for they had little ones daily) made greater havoc than the Earthquake itself.

By an Account dated the 23rd of September following, almost half the People, who escap'd the Port-Royal, were since dead of a malignant Fever, from the Change of Air, want of dry Houses, warm Lodging, proper Medicines, and other Conveniences.

Dr. Morley observes that this sickness (supposed to proceed from the hurtful Vapours belched from the many Openings in the Earth) spread all over Jamaica, and became so general that few escaped it. 'Tis thought it swept away, in many parts of the

We shall conclude the whole with remarks on the weather, both before and after the Earthquake. Dr. Morley observes that the year 1692 began with very dry and hot weather, which continued till May, when there was very blowing weather, and much rain till the end of the month. From that time till the Earthquake happened, it was

90

excessively hot, calm, and dry. We learn from another hand that the weather was much hotter after the Earthquake than before, and that there appeared such an innumerable quantity of mosquitoes as had never been seen in the island till then.

1694

The French Attack: Admiral Du Casse and the Invasion of Jamaica

In the midst of the Nine Years' War (1688–1697), longstanding hostilities between France and England reached Jamaican shores. In 1694, French Admiral Jean-Baptiste du Casse led a devastating assault on the island, launching one of the most formidable invasions Jamaica had faced since the English conquest in 1655.

A Vulnerable Island

After the 1692 earthquake sank much of Port Royal and weakened its coastal defenses, fears grew that the island was vulnerable to attack—particularly along the eastern coast. It was believed that any foreign enemy could bypass the slowly rebuilding defenses of Port Royal by landing troops east of the city, along the unguarded shores of St. Thomas and the Liguanea Plain.

This fear became reality in 1694, when Admiral Du Casse sailed from Saint-Domingue (present-day Haiti and the Dominican Republic) with a fleet carrying over 3,000 French troops.

91

Fortunately for the English, they were forewarned. The warning came from a British naval officer, Captain Elliott, who had been imprisoned by the French in Saint-Domingue. After escaping by canoe, he arrived in Jamaica on May 31 and alerted the authorities of the impending attack. The colony quickly mobilized, reinforcing the defensive guns at Port Royal and a small outpost at the eastern entrance of the harbor—today known as Rockfort.

The French Invasion

Within days, Du Casse's fleet, some 3,000 troops strong, anchored at Cow Bay, just north of the Yallahs River in eastern Jamaica. The invaders launched a destructive campaign through St. Thomas and St. Andrew, laying waste to plantations and property. After regrouping, the French sailed along the southern coast and attempted to land again at Carlisle Bay in Clarendon, aiming to strike at Spanish Town from the west.

But at Carlisle Bay, they were met by a force of just 250 Jamaican militiamen—outnumbered more than ten to one. Despite the odds, the militia mounted a fierce defense. In a remarkable display of courage and tactical skill, they repelled the French advance. Du Casse's forces suffered nearly 700 casualties before retreating.

Though the eastern parishes sustained heavy property damage and loss of life, Clarendon was spared. Many of its residents had already fled inland, reducing civilian casualties.

Aftermath and Significance

The 1694 French invasion marked one of the most serious military incursions to Jamaica during the colonial period. While the raid exposed weaknesses in the island's defenses, the resilience of the Jamaican militia—alongside timely intelligence

—proved decisive in preserving English control of the colony.

The event also underscored the ongoing geopolitical struggles of the era. Jamaica's strategic value in the Caribbean made it a continual target for rival empires, and it spurred renewed efforts to strengthen coastal defenses and build a more battle-ready militia.

Part 4

1700 – 1800: The Growth of the Plantation Economy and Resistance

The 18th century cemented Jamaica's status as the jewel of Britain's Caribbean colonies, with sugar plantations dominating the landscape. The brutal system of slavery fueled immense wealth for plantation owners but also intensified resistance. Maroon communities, formed by escaped slaves, waged persistent guerrilla warfare against British forces, leading to treaties that secured their semi-autonomous status. Enslaved uprisings and growing abolitionist sentiment in Britain signaled that change was on the horizon, setting the stage for major conflicts over the future of slavery.

1700s

Turn of a New Century

By the dawn of the 18th century, Jamaica had become a cornerstone of the British colonial economy, producing nearly 20% of the world's sugar supply. The number of sugar estates expanded from just 57 in 1673 to nearly 430 by the end of the First Maroon War in 1740. As sugar plantations multiplied, so too did the island's dependence on enslaved African labor, with the slave population growing rapidly throughout the century.

Although the Treaty of Madrid (1670) had formally ended hostilities between England and Spain and acknowledged England's control over Jamaica, Spain continued to be viewed as a potential threat. The political landscape of Europe remained volatile, and each new war between European powers risked reigniting conflict in the Caribbean. Spanish resentment over the loss of Jamaica lingered, and Spanish privateers — sometimes unofficially sanctioned — harassed British shipping and settlements. Moreover, Jamaica's flourishing illicit trade with Spanish colonies, especially through smuggling British goods into Spanish America, further provoked tensions.

At home, the island's plantation economy brought great wealth to England, especially to absentee landowners who managed their estates from afar. However, not all planters thrived. Smaller landowners, unable to compete with the larger sugar estates, increasingly diversified into crops like coffee, cotton, and indigo. By the late 1700s, coffee production was booming and began to rival sugar as a key export.

But Jamaica's success came at a devastating human cost. The brutality of slavery underpinned its prosperity, with enslaved people enduring inhumane treatment, backbreaking labor, and violent repression. As the century progressed, civil unrest grew. Rebellions, resistance, and Maroon activity all pointed to a society on edge—one built on a fragile foundation of exploitation.

1703

Port Royal Destroyed by Fire

On January 9, 1703, eleven years after the earthquake, disaster struck Port Royal once again when a fire broke out in a warehouse and quickly engulfed the town. Fueled by large quantities of gunpowder and flammable materials and exacerbated by narrow streets and tightly packed buildings, the inferno was unstoppable. The flames leapt from building to building, and by midnight, Port Royal lay in ruins. A lone boat master's log recorded the event succinctly: "Port Royal burnt, all but the Castle."

In the aftermath, a contentious proposal emerged to relocate all commercial activity to the burgeoning city of Kingston. Citing Kingston's perceived health and safety advantages, merchants favored the move. However, seamen and sailors argued vehemently against it, fearing the difficulties their ships would face navigating Kingston's harbor. The debate raged on, with both sides fiercely defending their positions. Ultimately, the proposal was abandoned, leaving both cities to develop in parallel—though Kingston would soon rise as the island's dominant commercial center.

Port Royal, however, never truly recovered from the devastating blow. Though some rebuilding efforts were made, the town never regained its former commercial glory. A string of devastating hurricanes—in 1712, 1722, 1726, and 1744—further crippled the town, extinguishing any lingering hopes of a full recovery. As the 18th century progressed, Port Royal's role shifted, gradually transforming into the principal British naval center in the Caribbean. Scarred by fire and battered by storms and earthquakes, the once-bustling port city found a new purpose as the empire's naval stronghold—leaving its golden age of commerce behind.

1718

Port Antonio Raided by French Privateers

In 1718, French privateers launched a daring assault on Port Antonio, capturing English merchant vessels and looting their cargo. This raid was not merely an act of piracy but a direct result of lingering tensions between France and England following the War of the Spanish Succession (1701–1714), a major European conflict over who would inherit the Spanish throne after the death of King Charles II of Spain. The war involved nearly all the major European powers and had significant global repercussions, including in the Caribbean and North America.

That conflict had erupted after the death of the childless Charles II of Spain in 1700, triggering a major European power struggle over the Spanish throne. Philip of Anjou, grandson of King Louis

XIV of France, was named heir, prompting opposition from a coalition led by England, the Dutch Republic, and Austria, who supported Archduke Charles of Austria.

Although the war officially ended in 1714, it left behind unresolved rivalries and economic competition, especially in the Caribbean. One common tactic used by both sides was privateering — the practice of licensing private ships to attack enemy commerce as a sanctioned act of war. These state-sanctioned pirates blurred the lines between warfare and piracy, especially in regions like the West Indies.

The raid on Port Antonio exemplified this shadow war. Though the conflict had officially ended, the rivalry between France and England continued to play out in the Caribbean. While not part of any official military campaign, the attack served to disrupt English trade and weaken British influence in the region. It also underscored the vulnerability of Jamaica's coastal towns and merchant vessels to foreign aggression and the enduring risks of colonial competition in the Caribbean.

1728

The First Maroon War

The First Maroon War (1728–1740) was a pivotal conflict in Jamaica's history, rooted in decades of shifting alliances, territorial disputes, and growing tensions between the British and the Maroons—self-liberated African communities that had established settlements in the island's mountainous interior.

When the British invaded Jamaica in 1655, they encountered fierce resistance—not just from the Spanish, but from African fighters who had escaped slavery under Spanish rule and established independent settlements in the island's rugged interior. These early Maroons initially fought alongside the Spanish in a failed effort to repel the English invaders. However, one prominent leader, Juan de Bolas, chose to switch allegiance and support the British — a decision that was deeply unpopular among other Maroon factions, but one that secured him land and formal recognition from the colonial authorities.

Despite this early cooperation, relations between the British and the Maroons remained hostile. As British colonial settlement expanded and the plantation economy grew, the Maroons were increasingly viewed as a threat to British control — especially as they began offering refuge to runaway slaves and resisting encroachments on their territory. Skirmishes and raids escalated over the decades, eventually erupting into full-scale warfare by the late 1720s.

The Maroons were divided into two main groups: the Leeward Maroons in the west, based in the Cockpit Country and led by Cudjoe, and the Windward Maroons in the east, occupying the Blue Mountains and led by figures such as Quao and Nanny. Both groups were highly skilled in guerrilla warfare and used their deep knowledge of the terrain to launch effective hit-and-run attacks on British settlements and plantations.

British forces responded with repeated military expeditions, but their efforts were frustrated by the Maroons' superior mobility and knowledge of the land. The conflict dragged on for over a decade.

There is no single documented event in 1728 that marked the beginning of the First Maroon War. Rather, the conflict appears to have been the culmination of years of growing resentment over land, freedom, and autonomy between the Maroons and the expanding planter class—a kind of "death by a thousand cuts." The Maroons were determined to exercise their rights to their land and their freedom, while the British increasingly saw their presence as an obstacle to realizing the full economic and territorial potential of the colony. This tension was intensified by a renewed British campaign to forcibly subdue the Maroons, particularly in the west. Governor Robert Hunter, seeking to assert greater control over the island's interior, is believed to have authorized a major military push against the Leeward Maroons under Cudjoe. This escalation provoked sustained resistance and ignited a protracted conflict that would last over a decade.

Phillip Thicknesse, a British military officer and administrator, later chronicled the war in his memoirs, offering rare insight into the strategies, negotiations, and social tensions that defined the conflict.

Several key events marked the progression and eventual end of the First Maroon War. Recognizing the futility of their military campaigns, the British began negotiations.

The Treaties That Ended the War

After years of unsuccessful military campaigns, the British opted for negotiation. However, the resolution of the conflict was not immediate. The staggered agreements reflected the complex dynamics between the British, the different Maroon factions, and the internal divisions within the Maroon leadership. Geographic separation, mistrust, and the independent nature of the Maroon communities contributed to the drawn-out conclusion of the war.

1739 – The Accompong Treaty: In 1739, Cudjoe, the Leeward Maroon leader, signed a treaty with the British. In return for land, semi-autonomous status, and certain freedoms, the Maroons agreed to stop harboring runaway slaves and to assist in suppressing future slave revolts. However, this deal was signed without consulting the Windward Maroons, led by Quao, the Windward Maroon military leader, and Nanny, their military and spiritual leader. This heightened tensions between the factions. The British likely hoped that securing a treaty with the Leeward Maroons would pressure the remaining factions to follow suit.

1739 (December) – Quao's Treaty: Ten months later, Quao, the Windward Maroon military leader, accepted a similar treaty. His decision to negotiate was partly influenced by the British military's ongoing presence and the strategic advantage of peace. However, Nanny refused the terms at first, believing they compromised the freedom and autonomy the Maroons had fought to preserve. This division briefly prolonged hostilities in the east.

1740 – Nanny's Agreement: Eventually, Nanny, the spiritual and military leader of the Windward Maroons, accepted the treaty terms, formally bringing the First Maroon War to an end. While her decision may have stemmed from mounting pressure and the need to protect her people from further conflict, the agreement also acknowledged the Maroons' resilience and forced the British to recognize their autonomy.

Today, Nanny is honored as a National Hero of Jamaica—Nanny of the Maroons—her name etched into the nation's history for her unmatched leadership, resistance, and courage during Jamaica's early struggles for freedom.

The First Maroon War was not just a military struggle — it was a defining moment in Jamaica's colonial history, symbolizing resistance, resilience, and the limits of imperial control. The staggered resolution serves as a reminder of the Maroons' determination to assert their independence and negotiate on their own terms.

The Terms of the Treaties

The 15 Articles of the Leeward Treaty

1. *That all hostilities shall cease on both sides forever.*

2. *That the said Captain Cudjoe, the rest of his captains, adherents and men, shall be forever hereafter in a perfect State of Freedom and Liberty, excepting those who have been taken by them, or fled to them within the two years last past, if such are willing to return to their said masters and owners, with full pardon and indemnity from their masters and owners for what is past. Provided always, that if they are not willing to return, they shall remain in subjection to captain Cudjoe, and in friendship with us, according to the form and tenor of this Treaty.*

3. *That they shall enjoy and possess for themselves and posterity forever, all the lands situated and lying between Trelawney Town and the Cockpits, to the amount of fifteen hundred acres, bearing Northwest from the said Trelawney Town.*

4. *That they shall have liberty to plant the said lands with coffee, ginger, tobacco and cotton, and breed cattle, hogs, goats, or any other stock, and dispose of the produce or the said commodities to the inhabitants of this island. Provided always, that when they bring the said commodities to market, they shall apply first to the Custos, or any other Magistrate of the respective Parishes where they expose their goods to sale, for licence to vend the same.*

5. *That Captain Cudjoe, and all his adherents, and people not in subjection to him, shall all live together within the bounds of Trelawney Town; and that they have liberty to hunt where they think fit, except within three miles of any Settlement, Crawl or Pen. Provided always, that in case the hunters of Captain Cudjoe, and those of other Settlements meet, then the hogs to be equally divided between both parties.*

6. *That said Captain Cudjoe and his successors, do use their best endeavours to take, kill, suppress or destroy, either by themselves or jointly, with any other number of men commanded by that service by his Excellency the Governor or Commander in Chief for the Time being, all Rebels wheresoever they be throughout this island, unless they submit to the same terms of accommodation granted to Captain Cudjoe, and his successors.*

7. *That in case this island be invaded by any foreign enemy, the said Captain Cudjoe, and his successors herein and after named, or to be appointed, shall then, upon notice given, immediately repair to any place the Governor for the Time being shall appoint, in order to repel the said invaders with his or their utmost force; and to submit to the orders of the Commander in Chief on that Occasion.*

8. *That if any White Man shall do any manner of injury to Captain Cudjoe, his successors, or any of his people, they shall apply to any commanding Officer or Magistrate in the neighbourhood for Justice; and in case Captain Cudjoe, or any of his people, shall do any injury to any white person, he shall submit himself or deliver up such offenders to justice.*

9. *That if any Negroes shall hereafter run away from their Master or Owners, and fall into Captain Cudjoe's Hands, they shall immediately be sent back to the Chief Magistrate of the next Parish where they are taken; and those that bring them are to be satisfied for their trouble, as Legislature shall appoint.*

10. *That all negroes taken since the raising of this Party by Captain Cudjoe's people, shall immediately be returned.*

11. *That Captain Cudjoe, and his successors, shall wait on his Excellency, or the Commander in Chief for the Time being, every year, if thereunto required.*

12. *That Captain Cudjoe, during his life, and the captains succeeding him, shall have full power to inflict any punishment they think proper for crimes committed by their men among themselves (death only excepted) in which case, if the captain thinks they deserve death, he shall be obliged to bring them before any Justice of the Peace, who shall order proceedings on their Trial equal to those of other free negroes.*

13. *That Captain Cudjoe with his people shall cut, clear, and keep open, large, and convenient roads from Trelawney Town to Westmoreland and St. James, and if possible to St. Elizabeth.*

14. *That two White Men to be nominated by his Excellency, or the Commander in Chief for the Time being, shall constantly live and reside with Captain Cudjoe and his successors, in order to maintain a friendly correspondence with the inhabitants of this Island.*

15. *That Captain Cudjoe shall, during his life, be Commander in Trelawney Town, after his Decease the command to devolve of his Brother Captain Accompong; and in case of his decease, on his next Brother Captain Johnny; and, failing him, Captain Cuffee shall succeed, who is to be succeeded by Captain Quaco, and after all their demises, the Governor or Commander in Chief for the Time being, shall appoint from Time to Time whom he thinks fit for that command.*

The 14 Articles of the Windward Treaty

1. *That all hostilities shall cease on both sides for ever, Amen.*

2. *That the said Captain Quao, and his people, shall have a certain quantity of land given to them, in order to raise provisions, hogs, fowls, goats, or whatever flock they may think proper, sugar canes excepted, saving for their hogs, and to have liberty to sell the same.*

3. That four white men shall constantly live and reside with them in their town, in order to keep a good correspondence with the inhabitants of this island.

4. That the said Captain Quao, and his people, shall be ready on all commands the governor, or the commander in chief for the time being, shall send him, to suppress and destroy all other party or parties of rebellious negroes, that now are or from time to time gather together to settle in any part of this island, and shall bring in such other negroes as shall from time to time run away from their respective owners, from the date of these articles.

5. That the said Captain Quao, and his people, shall also be ready to assist his Excellency the governor for the time being, in case of any invasion, and shall put himself, with all his people that are able to bear arms, under the command of the general or commander of such forces, appointed by his Excellency to defend the island from the said invasion.

6. That the said Captain Quao, and all his people, shall be in subjection to his Excellency the governor for the time being; and the said Captain Quao shall, once every year or oftener, appear before the governor, if thereunto required.

7. That in case any of the hunters belonging to the inhabitants of this island, and the hunters belonging to Captain Quao, should meet in order to hinder disputes, Captain Quao will order his people to let the inhabitants hunters have the hog.

8. That in case Captain Quao, or his people, shall take up run away negroes that shall abscond from their respective owners, and shall be paid for so doing as the legislature shall appoint.

9. That in case Captain Quao, and his people, should be disturbed by a greater number of rebels than he is able to fight, that then he shall be assisted by as many white people as the governor for the time being shall think proper.

10. That in case any of the negroes belonging o Captain Quao

shall be guilty of any crime or crimes that may deserve death, he shall deliver him up to the next magistrate, in order to be tried as other negroes are; but small crimes he may punish himself.

11. *That in case any white man, or other the inhabitants of this island, shall disturb or annoy any of the people, hogs, flock, or whatever goods may belong to the said Captain Quao, or any of his people, when they come down to the settlements to vend the same, upon due complaint made to a magistrate, he or they shall have justice done them.*

12. *That neither Captain Quao, nor any of his people, shall bring any hogs, fowls, or any stock or provisions, to sell to the inhabitants, without a ticket from under the hand of one or more of the white men residing in their town.*

13. *That Captain Quao, nor any of his people, shall hunt within three miles of any settlement.*

14. *That in case Captain Quao should die, that then the command of his people shall descend to Captain Thomboy; and at his death to descend to Captain Apong; and at his death Captain Blackwall shall succeed; and at his death Clash shall succeed; and, when he dies, the governor or commander in chief for the time being shall appoint whom he thinks proper.*

—*Source: National Library of Jamaica*

The Differences Between the Treaties

On close examination of the terms, it is clear that the treaties were inequitable, favoring the Leeward Maroons. This begs the question: why? The answer may lie in the British desire to reward the Leeward Maroons for agreeing to an early settlement, while imposing a punitive agreement on the Windward Maroons for their prolonged resistance. Yet this imbalance carried further consequences. By offering lesser terms to the Windward Maroons, the British risked deepening divisions between the factions. Leaders like Quao and Nanny were already angered by the Leeward Maroons' unilateral decision to sign a treaty without their knowledge. The inequitable terms that followed not only reflected British strategy but also threatened to fracture Maroon unity in the aftermath of the war.

Land Grants

The most glaring disparity is evident in the allocation of land. Under the Leeward Treaty, Captain Cudjoe and his followers were granted 1,500 acres, providing ample space for cultivation and self-sufficiency. Notably, the agreement did not restrict the planting of sugar cane, a crop closely tied to the island's plantation economy. In contrast, the Windward Maroons, led by Captain Quao and Nanny, received a vague promise of a "certain quantity of land." Historical records suggest they were granted only 500 acres—a third of what the Leeward Maroons secured. Compounding the inequity, the Windward Treaty expressly forbade the cultivation of sugar cane, except for feeding livestock. This stipulation prevented them from engaging in the most lucrative agricultural practice of the time, further limiting their economic autonomy.

White Cohabitation Mandate

The disparity extended to the issue of oversight. The Leeward Maroons were required to accept the presence of two white men appointed by the governor, ostensibly to maintain peace and ensure compliance. However, the Windward Maroons faced double that number, with four white overseers stationed within their community. This heightened level of surveillance suggests a greater degree of mistrust towards the Windward Maroons, who had maintained fierce resistance against British forces. The increased oversight served as a constant reminder of colonial control and undermined the authority of their own leaders.

Trade Regulation

Trade regulations further illustrate the imbalance between the two agreements. While both factions faced restrictions, the Leeward Treaty required a license from local authorities for the sale of hogs, fowls, or other provisions to colonial inhabitants. This allowed some degree of external economic engagement. The Windward Maroons, however, faced an additional layer of control. Their licenses could only be granted by one or more of the white overseers residing among them. This meant their limited economic activities were subject to the direct scrutiny of those tasked with monitoring them, further curbing their economic independence.

Hunting Rights

Perhaps the most punitive measure concerned hunting rights. In an agrarian society where hunting provided a vital source of food, the terms imposed on the Windward Maroons were particularly harsh. The Leeward Maroons were required to share the spoils of a hunt equally with settlers if their paths crossed. While this was a concession to British settlers, it at least retained a measure of fairness. The Windward Maroons, however, were stripped of even this right. If their hunters encountered settlers, the treaty stipulated that the settlers would claim the entire bounty. This symbolic act of dominance ensured that the Windward Maroons were continually reminded of their subjugation.

A Fragile Truce

In essence, the treaties' inequities reflect the British strategy of divide and rule. The Leeward Maroons, through their early capitulation, secured relatively favorable terms, while the Windward Maroons, who resisted until the end, were subjected to harsher restrictions. The treaties were not merely peace agreements; they were tools of colonial control, designed to reward compliance and punish defiance. This legacy of inequality would continue to shape the relationship between the Maroons and the British authorities in the years that followed.

The inequities between the treaties not only reflected the British intent to reward early cooperation and punish prolonged resistance but also planted the seeds for future instability. While the agreements brought a temporary peace, the resentment they fostered, particularly among the Windward Maroons, likely contributed to lingering divisions.

Ironically, it was not the Windward factions that would rise in rebellion decades later, but the Leeward Maroons. The Second Maroon War of 1795 saw the Trelawny Town Maroons — a Leeward group that had once accepted more favorable treaty terms — take up arms against the British. While the immediate causes of that conflict were different, the complex legacy of the treaties may have played a role in shaping the tensions that resurfaced. The British practice of granting unequal concessions and using divide-and-rule tactics to maintain control may have ultimately eroded even the fragile loyalty of those they had once rewarded.

In the end, the treaties stand not just as documents of negotiated peace, but as lasting symbols of both resistance and manipulation in Jamaica's colonial history.

1737

Coffee: The Birth of the Coffee Industry

The introduction of coffee to Jamaica is credited to Sir Nicholas Lawes, who served as the island's governor from 1718 to 1722. In 1728, Lawes received coffee plants as a gift from the Governor of Martinique, a French colony where coffee cultivation had already begun with plants sent by King Louis XV. After receiving the plants, Sir Nicholas Lawes established the first coffee cultivation at his Temple Hall Estate, located in St. Andrew Parish.

Temple Hall was originally a sugar estate but, under Lawes's stewardship, it transformed into an agricultural experimentation site, where various crops were tested for their potential success in Jamaica's climate. By 1737, nine years after the initial planting, the coffee trees had matured, and production had expanded enough to support exports, marking the beginning of Jamaica's coffee industry.

Throughout the 18th and 19th centuries, Jamaican coffee, particularly the beans grown in the Blue Mountains, gained a reputation for superior quality and smooth flavor. The British, always eager to reduce dependence on foreign goods, heavily promoted Jamaican coffee as a rival to Brazilian and Yemeni varieties. By the early 1800s, plantations across St. Andrew, Portland, and St. Thomas supplied beans directly to London's high-end coffee houses.

However, the industry suffered setbacks in the late 19th century, as sugar planters took over much of the island's fertile land. Many former coffee estates were abandoned, though small-scale farming persisted. By the 20th century, interest in high-quality, specialty coffee revived the industry, and today, Jamaican Blue Mountain Coffee remains one of the most expensive and sought-after coffees in the world.

1744

Pimento: The Spice That Built an Industry

Centuries before European conquest, the Taíno people cultivated pimento (allspice), valuing it for its bold flavor, medicinal properties, and ability to preserve food. When the British seized control of Jamaica in 1655, they quickly recognized the spice's commercial potential. By 1744, pimento had emerged as one of the island's most valuable exports.

What Makes Jamaican Pimento Unique?

Pimento is indigenous to Jamaica and parts of Central America, but Jamaica remains the world's primary producer. The island's unique terroir—a combination of limestone-rich soil, tropical climate, and high-altitude terrain—produces pimento berries with a higher essential oil content than those grown elsewhere. These oils, including eugenol, which gives allspice its characteristic warm, clove-like aroma, make Jamaican pimento more potent and aromatic than varieties grown in other regions.

Unlike other spice-producing countries where trees are heavily cultivated or altered for higher yields, Jamaican pimento grows naturally in the wild, primarily in the central and western parishes such as St. Elizabeth, Manchester, and Trelawny. The trees thrive in limestone-rich soil, which further enhances the concentration of essential oils. This natural growth process preserves the distinct flavor profile that has made Jamaican allspice the gold standard in the global spice trade.

Pimento's Role in Global Trade

By the mid-1700s, Jamaica had become the world's largest supplier of pimento, commanding a significant share of the global spice trade and exporting dried berries to Britain, Spain, and North America. The spice became particularly valuable in European and Caribbean cuisine, playing a crucial role in sausages, pickling, marinades, and baked goods. One of its most essential functions was in meat preservation, as its antimicrobial properties helped slow spoilage in the days before refrigeration.

While pimento established itself as a key player in global trade, its significance extended far beyond the export markets. Unlike sugar, which required large-scale plantations and enslaved labor, pimento cultivation was less labor-intensive, allowing for smaller, independent farms. After emancipation in 1838, many formerly enslaved Jamaicans turned to pimento farming as a means of self-sufficiency, helping to sustain Jamaica's emerging peasant economy. Today, Jamaica remains one of the world's leading producers of pimento, a testament to its centuries-old spice trade and the resilience of its people.

Cocoa: The Forgotten Gold of the 18th Century

In 1747, cocoa (the raw ingredient for chocolate) became a promising export crop in Jamaica. Spanish settlers had introduced cocoa trees in the 1500s, but it wasn't until the British era that production expanded significantly.

By the late 18th century, Jamaican cocoa was exported alongside sugar and coffee, supplying Britain's growing chocolate industry. Chocolate, then consumed as a luxurious drink, was popular in London's elite social circles. Jamaica's climate, particularly in Clarendon, St. Mary, and Portland, proved ideal for growing high-quality cocoa beans.

Cocoa plantations thrived through the 19th century, but by the early 20th century, competition from West Africa—particularly Ghana—led to a sharp decline in Jamaica's cocoa industry. Many farmers abandoned the crop in favor of bananas and other commodities.

Though no longer a dominant export, cocoa production never disappeared entirely. Today, small-scale farmers are reviving Jamaica's fine-flavored cocoa, which is once again gaining international recognition for its rich, fruity notes and superior quality.

Formation of the Counties

Jamaica was formally divided into three counties in 1758:

Cornwall: The westernmost county, named after the English county of Cornwall.

Middlesex: The central county, named after the English county of Middlesex.

Surrey: The easternmost county, named after the English county of Surrey.

The purpose of the division was primarily to facilitate the administration of the judicial system, following the model of the British county court system. However, these counties never held significant administrative power and are now largely historical designations.

While the counties were established in 1758, the island had been divided into parishes since the English took control in 1655. The parishes were the main units of local government and remain so today. There were initially only seven parishes, but the number fluctuated over time until it was finally settled at the current 14 in 1867.

The Question of a 15th Parish

At the time of this book's publication, legislation to create a 15th parish was making its way through the parliamentary process, marking the first creation of a new parish in over a century. If approved, Portmore and its immediate surroundings would be separated from St. Catherine, reducing the size and jurisdiction of that parish, and granting Portmore administrative autonomy. The proposal reflects Portmore's significant population growth and its increasing economic and political importance within the Kingston Metropolitan Area.

1760

Tacky's Rebellion

Tacky's War, also known as the Easter Rebellion of 1760, was one of the largest and most significant slave uprisings in Jamaica during the 18th century. It was a direct response to the brutal conditions of the plantation system and the relentless exploitation of enslaved Africans. The rebellion was named after Tacky, an enslaved Akan African man who emerged as one of its principal leaders. Drawing upon his experiences as a former chief in West Africa, Tacky's leadership and military knowledge shaped the course of the rebellion.

What began as a localized rebellion in St. Mary Parish quickly spread across the island, with enslaved Africans in multiple parishes rising up in pursuit of freedom. The scale and speed of the revolt have led some historians to suggest that the widespread uprisings were evidence of a broader, coordinated plan. Others, however, argue that the rebellion in St. Mary acted as a catalyst, inspiring enslaved people in other regions to rebel.

A contemporaneous account from Thomas Thistlewood's diary provides a vivid perspective on the immediate fear and confusion that spread among the white population. Thistlewood, an Englishman who arrived in Jamaica in 1750, spent years as an overseer before becoming a plantation owner. Known for keeping meticulous diaries, he recorded the details of his daily life, offering a candid and unfiltered view of his interactions with enslaved people, his management of plantation labor, and his observations on colonial society. Historians have since used his accounts to gain valuable insight into the complexities of life in 18th-century Jamaica, particularly the attitudes and fears of the planter class.

During Tacky's War, Thistlewood's detailed observations not only document the violent suppression that followed but also highlight the panic that consumed colonial society. Plantation owners across the island grew increasingly anxious as rumors of further insurrections circulated. His accounts reveal the rapid mobilization of militias and the harsh retaliatory measures taken against suspected rebels, illustrating the widespread fear that gripped Jamaica in the aftermath of the rebellion.

The rebellion began on Easter Sunday in St. Mary Parish when Tacky and his followers attacked the Fort Haldane garrison. After seizing firearms and ammunition, they killed the soldiers on duty and launched a series of assaults on nearby plantations. The insurgents moved swiftly, destroying property, killing enslavers, and liberating fellow enslaved Africans. Their efforts sent shockwaves through the colony, leading enslaved people across Jamaica to join the rebellion. Uprisings erupted in multiple parishes, including St. Thomas in the East, St. John, Kingston, St. James, Hanover, and Westmoreland. In Westmoreland, the scale of the rebellion nearly matched that of St. Mary, further suggesting that the uprising may have been part of a wider resistance effort. Reports from the time estimate that over 50 whites were killed, and nearly 400 enslaved Africans lost their lives, either in battle or through the brutal punishments that followed.

Thistlewood's diary also provides a chilling account of Tacky's capture and death. After days of pursuit by militias and Maroon forces—who were bound by their 1739 treaty with the British to suppress rebellions—Tacky was finally cornered in the forest. Davy, a Maroon sharpshooter, reportedly fired the fatal shot that ended Tacky's life. In a brutal display meant to serve as a warning to others, Tacky's severed head was displayed on a pole. Thistlewood described the grim scene, emphasizing the colonial authorities' ruthless determination to suppress further revolts. Despite Tacky's death, fear lingered. Rumors of continued resistance and conspiracies fueled further paranoia, leading to widespread executions and violent reprisals.

The rebellion also highlighted the strategic acumen of the rebels, who effectively used guerrilla tactics and their intimate knowledge of the island's mountainous terrain to evade capture. The uprising exposed the fragility of British control and underscored the persistent resistance of enslaved Africans in Jamaica.

More than seventy years later, this spirit of defiance resurfaced in the Christmas Rebellion of 1831, which became a decisive factor in the push toward emancipation.

—Primary Sources: In Miserable Slavery—Thistlewood in Jamaica 1750-86
Douglas Hall
Tacky's Revolt: The Story of an Atlantic Slave War by Vincent Brown.

The Second Maroon War (1795-1796)

The treaty between the Maroons and the British, signed at the end of the First Maroon War, began to fray over time as disputes arose over its terms. While the Leeward Maroons had initially benefited from more favorable conditions, including greater land allocations and fewer restrictions, these advantages became increasingly meaningless as sugar plantations expanded into lands they considered their own. The British also imposed restrictions on Maroon activities like hunting and farming, undermining their self-sufficiency and further fueling their discontent. With the settlers' encroachment effectively violating the spirit of the agreements, the bitterness that had likely been simmering for decades erupted into open conflict. The boundaries of Maroon territories, often unclear and contested, only intensified the clashes with neighboring plantations and settlements.

The Second Maroon War primarily involved the Leeward Maroons of Trelawny Town, whose long-standing frustrations with the British erupted into conflict. In contrast, the role of Accompong Town, another Leeward Maroon community, remains a subject of historical debate. Some accounts suggest that they remained neutral, adhering to the terms of their earlier treaty with the British, while others indicate that individuals from Accompong may have supported the British, though not necessarily as active combatants. Regardless of their exact role, Accompong's decision shaped the course of the war and further complicated the relationship between the Maroons and the British authorities.

The breaking point that sparked the war came in 1795 when two Maroons, allegedly accused of stealing pigs, were publicly flogged in Montego Bay by order of a British court. For the Maroons, the punishment was a deeply humiliating violation of their autonomy and a stark reminder of their diminished status under British rule. Coupled with ongoing grievances over land encroachment and perceived betrayal, the incident ignited widespread outrage. The sense of injustice reverberated through Trelawny Town, ultimately leading to the outbreak of the Second Maroon War.

The outbreak of the war was marked by a series of skirmishes between Maroons and British troops in Trelawny Town (now known as Maroon Town). The Maroons, skilled in guerrilla warfare and intimately familiar with the terrain, launched surprise attacks and ambushes, effectively utilizing the rugged Jamaican landscape to their advantage. The British colonial authorities, facing a formidable enemy, deployed significant military force, including regular troops, militia, and bloodhounds imported from Cuba.

Despite their superior firepower and resources, the British struggled to adapt to the Maroons' guerrilla tactics, and the war eventually reached a stalemate. Negotiations ensued, and a truce was agreed. The exact terms of the truce remain a subject of historical debate. While the Maroons were believed to have agreed to surrender their arms and leaders in exchange for amnesty and the promise of continued freedom within their territory, the British did not necessarily uphold these agreements in good faith. Growing fears of further uprisings, combined with pressure from planters and colonial authorities, ultimately influenced their actions. The breach of the truce further deepened the distrust between the Maroons and the colonial government, leaving a legacy of unresolved grievances.

Regardless of the specifics of the truce, the new governor of Jamaica, Alexander Lindsay, Earl of Balcarres, under pressure from panicked planters and a hostile Assembly, acted against the spirit of the agreement and deported over 500 Maroons—including men, women, and children—to Nova Scotia in 1796. Years later, facing harsh conditions and broken promises, the deportees were relocated to Sierra Leone by British authorities overseeing resettlement efforts.

This decision was likely driven by a combination of factors, including fear of the Maroons' continued resistance and a desire to eliminate a potential threat to the colonial order. The deportation of the Maroons stands as a stark reminder of the broken promises and injustices inflicted upon them by the colonial authorities.

Prominent Figures

Colonel Montague James and Leonard Parkinson were key figures in the Maroon resistance during the Second Maroon War, leading the fight against British forces.

Colonel Montague James, the leader of the Trelawny Town Maroons, played a significant role in organizing and commanding the resistance. Known for his leadership and tactical prowess, he led guerrilla campaigns against the British, using the dense forests and mountainous terrain to the Maroons' advantage. Despite being outnumbered and facing harsh conditions, James's resilience and determination prolonged the conflict and frustrated the British military. When the war reached a stalemate, he participated in the truce negotiations, seeking to secure the best possible terms for his people.

Leonard Parkinson, a captain among the Trelawny Town Maroons, became widely known for his daring raids and effective use of guerrilla tactics. His knowledge of the Jamaican landscape allowed him to lead ambushes and evade capture, making him a formidable opponent to the British forces. While his role in the formal negotiations is less documented, Parkinson's leadership on the battlefield exemplified the Maroons' fierce determination to defend their autonomy. His reputation as a courageous fighter made him a lasting symbol of resistance in Jamaican history.

1796: Some Trelawny Town Maroons Deported to Nova Scotia

Following a bitter conflict with the British, a group of Trelawny Town Maroons, comprising men, women, and children, were forcibly relocated to Halifax, Nova Scotia, around July 1796.

Numbering somewhere between 500 and 600, the Maroons arrived in July 1796. Upon their arrival, some were employed in fortifying Citadel Hill and working on other military and infrastructure projects. At Citadel Hill, they constructed one of the bastions, later known as the "Maroon Bastion."

Initially, the Maroons lived in temporary housing, including tents, barracks, and repurposed structures on the Citadel's grounds, as well as in barns on the Governor's property. Governor John Wentworth, aiming to promote agriculture, allotted them land in the Preston area. However, the plan proved unsustainable due to dissatisfaction with the quality of the land, the harsh northern climate, and attempts to convert them to Christianity.

Disputes emerged within the Maroon community, reflecting growing dissatisfaction with their treatment in Nova Scotia and the hardships of adapting to the harsh climate and limited opportunities. Led by prominent Maroon leader James Palmer, some settled in Boydville, a small community about 14 miles from Preston. While the Boydville Maroons attempted to adapt, others in Preston continued to petition for relief or relocation.

In response to this unrest—and recalling an earlier relocation of Black Loyalists to West Africa—British officials proposed resettlement in the colony of Sierra Leone in Africa. The move was organized by the Sierra Leone Company, a British philanthropic and commercial organization founded in 1791 by abolitionists, including Granville Sharp. The company had established Freetown, now the capital city of Sierra Leone, in 1792 as a settlement for freed Black Loyalists and formerly enslaved Africans. By 1800, it was still managing the colony, offering land and governance under British oversight.

The offer to the Maroons was presented as a solution, but in reality, it reflected the lack of viable alternatives. They were barred from returning to Jamaica, and their situation in Nova Scotia had become increasingly untenable. In August 1800, over 500 Maroons were resettled in Sierra Leone under the supervision of the Sierra Leone Company. A small number chose to remain in Nova Scotia, likely due to personal ties or the hope of improved conditions.

Although their stay in Nova Scotia was brief, the Maroons contributed to the region's cultural landscape, and their legacy is preserved in the names of Maroon Hill and Citadel Hill (Maroon Bastion).

Maroon Hill, a small community located in the Sackville area of Nova Scotia, is named after the Maroons who settled there, including those led by James Palmer, who were part of the

Boydville settlement. The name serves as a reminder of their presence and contributions to the area.

Both of these places bear the name "Maroon" to honor and remember the history and legacy of the Jamaican Maroons in Nova Scotia. This ensures that their story is not forgotten and that their presence in the region is acknowledged and recognized.

Their story stands as a testament to resilience, cultural preservation, and the ongoing struggle for self-determination.

Part 5

1800 – 1865: Emancipation, Free Villages, and Social Change

The early 19th century brought dramatic shifts to Jamaica's social and economic structure. Slave revolts, particularly the Christmas Rebellion of 1831, accelerated the push for emancipation. Slavery was officially abolished in 1834, with full freedom granted in 1838. The period that followed saw the rise of free villages, as formerly enslaved people sought autonomy and land ownership.

These changes coincided with a steady decline in the plantation system. Sugar estates had grown from 651 in 1768 to 710 in 1789, peaking at 859 in 1804. By 1834, the number had fallen to 646, then dropped to just 330 by 1854, a 62% decline from the peak—reflecting the collapse of the old slave-based economy.
— *Number of sugar plantations and estates in Jamaica 1768–1854, Statista Research Department, 1978.*

However, tensions between the Black majority and the colonial elite persisted, culminating in the Morant Bay Rebellion of 1865—a watershed moment that led to direct Crown rule and a new phase of governance.

1804

The Haitian Revolution Causes Concerns in Jamaica

In 1804, Haiti declared its independence, becoming the first Black republic in the Western Hemisphere and marking the successful conclusion of the Haitian Revolution (1791–1804). The revolution was a seismic event that reverberated across the Caribbean, sending shockwaves through Jamaica's planter class. For years, the Haitian enslaved population had fought and defeated the French, ultimately overthrowing their oppressors and establishing a free nation. To enslaved people in Jamaica, Haiti's victory stood as a beacon of hope—proof that resistance could lead to freedom. To British colonial authorities and plantation owners, however, it was a chilling reminder of the fragility of their own dominance.

The Impact on Jamaica

News of Haiti's independence spread rapidly across the island, inspiring hope and determination among the enslaved. Stories of the revolution circulated, fueling the belief that rebellion was not only possible but could succeed. Though no large-scale revolt erupted in Jamaica in 1804, the atmosphere of defiance was palpable, and the fear of an uprising loomed large in the minds of the planters.

Increased Security

In response, Jamaican authorities swiftly bolstered their defenses. The militia forces were expanded, and British military presence was strengthened. Plantation patrols grew more vigilant, and the colonial government introduced harsher punishments for acts of resistance. Any sign of dissent was met with brutal suppression, as the authorities sought to eliminate even the faintest echo of Haitian influence.

Call for Reforms

The anxiety among planters also stirred broader discussions about the future of slavery. Some British officials, witnessing the devastating consequences of the Haitian Revolution for the French economy, began to question the sustainability of the plantation system. Although most Jamaican planters stubbornly clung to their reliance on enslaved labor, the events in Haiti intensified the growing abolitionist movement in Britain. The fear that similar uprisings could erupt across the British Caribbean forced planters to reckon with the possibility that their hold on power might not last forever.

The Haitian Revolution served as a powerful harbinger of what could happen in Jamaica, reinforcing the idea that enslaved people would fight for freedom and adding weight to abolitionist arguments in Britain. Over time, these pressures, along with shifting economic and moral concerns, would play a role in shaping Britain's policies on the transatlantic slave trade.

The Abolition of the Transatlantic Slave Trade

By the early 19th century, the transatlantic slave trade—once seen as essential to Britain's economic success—was facing growing opposition. For decades, abolitionists had exposed its brutal realities, drawing attention to the horrific conditions aboard slave ships and the suffering of millions forcibly taken from Africa. Campaigns led by figures like William Wilberforce, Thomas Clarkson, and Olaudah Equiano had stirred public sentiment, forcing the British government to confront the moral and economic costs of the trade.

At the same time, Britain's industrial economy was evolving. The sugar industry, though still profitable, was declining in dominance, and some policymakers began to question whether slavery was truly sustainable. International pressures also played a role—Haiti's successful revolution had proven that enslaved people would not remain passive, and the fear of similar uprisings loomed over the British Caribbean.

Faced with these mounting pressures, Parliament took its first major step toward dismantling the transatlantic slave trade. In 1807, the Abolition of the Slave Trade Act was passed, making it illegal to buy, sell, or transport enslaved people across the British Empire. While this marked a significant victory for abolitionists, it did not end slavery itself. Enslaved people in Jamaica remained in bondage, and the internal trade of enslaved people within the island continued, leaving their daily lives unchanged.

On the island, the response from the planter class was one of defiance and fear. Many were unwilling to accept even this small step toward abolition, and some continued illicit trading, smuggling enslaved Africans into Jamaica despite the new law. Others turned to internal slave breeding to maintain their labor force. Meanwhile, plantation owners tightened their grip on the enslaved population, enforcing harsher punishments and restrictions to prevent resistance.

Yet, for those suffering under the system, 1807 marked a shift—a crack in the foundation of the institution that had ruled their lives for generations. It was proof that change, however slow, was possible.

1814

The Peak of Jamaican Sugar Production

By 1814, Jamaica remained the world's largest sugar producer, generating a staggering £34 million in revenue (approximately £2.3 billion today using the Bank of England's CPI calculator). However, pressures on the plantation system were beginning to emerge. The island's economy was built primarily on the backs of enslaved Africans, along with smaller numbers of indentured laborers and free workers. Yet beneath this facade of prosperity, resistance simmered. Enslaved people fought for freedom through both open revolts and subtle acts of defiance.

The wealth flowing from Jamaica's sugar fields did not remain on the island. It fueled Britain's economic expansion, particularly in cities like Liverpool and Bristol, which thrived on the sugar trade. Bristol's refineries processed vast quantities of raw sugar, transforming it into the refined product consumed across Britain. Liverpool, once a hub for the transatlantic slave trade, adapted by focusing on financing, shipping, and plantation investments, continuing to profit from Caribbean slavery even after the abolition of the slave trade in 1807. Banks, insurance companies, and merchants in both cities built their fortunes on the back of Jamaican sugar, further entrenching Britain's dependence on slavery.

While no large-scale uprising had occurred in Jamaica, British officials remained on high alert for signs of rebellion. The memory of the Second Maroon War (1795–96) and Tacky's War (1760) loomed large, demonstrating that enslaved Africans were willing to fight and die for their freedom. The Haitian Revolution of 1804 remained a stark warning of what could happen. Haiti, the first Black republic, had overthrown French rule and abolished slavery—proving that enslaved people could successfully rise up and seize their freedom.

Shifting Winds in the Empire

Although the British Empire still depended on Jamaican sugar, change was on the horizon. The horrors of the transatlantic slave trade had sparked growing opposition in Britain, leading to the Abolition of the Slave Trade Act in 1807. However, slavery itself remained legal, and plantation owners were determined to maintain their grip on power.

At the same time, global conflicts, particularly the Napoleonic Wars (1803–1815), disrupted Britain's economy. Napoleon's dominance over continental Europe disrupted traditional trade routes, but Britain adapted by redirecting Caribbean sugar exports to its own markets and neutral nations. Meanwhile, naval warfare made transatlantic shipping increasingly dangerous, adding further pressure to the plantation economy.

Jamaica's sugar empire was still standing—but cracks had begun to form.

1823

The Anti-Slavery Society and the Push for Emancipation

In 1823, abolitionists William Wilberforce, Thomas Clarkson, and Thomas Fowell Buxton founded *The Society for the Mitigation and Gradual Abolition of Slavery Throughout the British Dominions*—commonly known as *The Anti-Slavery Society*—pushing for the gradual abolition of slavery. While the slave trade had ended in 1807, slavery itself remained intact, and conditions in Jamaica were as harsh and oppressive as ever. The Society intensified public pressure and lobbied Parliament, leading to the British government's Amelioration Proposals, aimed at improving conditions for the enslaved.

The proposals included:

- Providing enslaved people with Sundays off and reducing their work hours.
- Ending the flogging of women and restricting corporal punishment.
- Allowing enslaved people to legally marry and maintain family structures.

- Increasing access to religious instruction through Christian missionaries.

However, these proposals faced fierce opposition from Jamaican planters, who refused to implement them. Many plantation owners believed that even minor improvements to the lives of the enslaved would undermine their control. Planters and their allies in Britain's Parliament lobbied aggressively to weaken or delay reforms, fearing that any concession would embolden further resistance. Despite mounting public pressure, the colonial government did little to enforce the proposals. For the enslaved, these measures did little to ease daily suffering, and many saw them as empty gestures.

Meanwhile, tensions were rising across the British colonies. That same year, the Demerara Rebellion erupted in British Guiana, where over 10,000 enslaved people revolted after believing their freedom was being withheld. Though swiftly suppressed, the rebellion unsettled British authorities and planters alike, highlighting the growing unrest in the Caribbean.

1831

The Baptist War Ignites a Turning Point

As the year 1831 drew to a close, unrest spread across Jamaica. Generations of enslaved people had endured the harsh realities of plantation life, while whispers of emancipation from Britain sparked hope and uncertainty. Among those determined to see freedom realized was Samuel Sharpe, a literate Baptist deacon respected within his community. Inspired by abolitionist ideals,

Sharpe devised a plan for a peaceful protest — a general strike intended to pressure plantation owners into granting better conditions and wages.

The strike was set to begin after the Christmas holidays, but tensions quickly escalated. On the night of December 27, 1831, a fire broke out at Kensington Estate in St. James. Whether accidental or deliberate, the blaze signaled the beginning of a larger rebellion. Plantations were set alight, and thousands of enslaved people across western Jamaica joined the uprising. The rebellion, later known as the Baptist War, became the largest in the island's history. While some rebels engaged in direct conflict, many followed Sharpe's vision of resistance through refusal to work.

The British responded swiftly and violently. Warships arrived to suppress the uprising, and local militias, composed largely of white planters, carried out brutal counterattacks. Within ten days, the rebellion was crushed, leaving destruction in its wake. An estimated 500 enslaved people lost their lives, not only in battle but also in the widespread executions that followed. Summary trials were held with little regard for justice, and punishment was severe.

Samuel Sharpe, who had hoped for peaceful resistance, was captured, tried, and sentenced to death. Before his execution in May 1832, he famously declared,

"I would rather die upon yonder gallows than live in slavery."
— Samuel Sharpe, May 1832

In the wake of the rebellion, white Jamaicans, consumed by fear and resentment, sought scapegoats. Missionaries who had supported and educated the enslaved population became the focus of violent reprisal. Baptist chapels were set ablaze, and missionary leaders faced intimidation, assault, and exile — their work condemned as seditious.

A Legacy of Change

The echoes of the Baptist War reverberated far beyond the shores of Jamaica, shaking the foundations of British society. For years, Parliament had engaged in protracted debates about the morality of slavery, but the rebellion laid bare the brutal reality and inherent instability of the system. The planters' long-held argument that enslaved people were content with their lot, or that gradual reforms would maintain peace, lay shattered amidst the burned-out estates.

Seizing the opportunity, abolitionists in Britain rallied public opinion and intensified their pressure on the government. The stories of courage, sacrifice, and the undeniable desire for freedom emanating from Jamaica forced Parliament to confront the urgency of the situation. In 1833, a mere year and a half after the rebellion, the British government finally passed the Slavery Abolition Act, a watershed moment that outlawed slavery throughout the British Empire.

The Baptist War, though born of oppression and quelled with violence, ultimately served as the final, irrefutable catalyst for emancipation. The blood and ashes of rebellion paved the path toward a new era, one in which the promise of freedom, however belated, finally began to dawn on the island of Jamaica.

Today, Samuel Sharpe is revered as a National Hero of Jamaica, his name forever etched in the annals of history as a symbol of courage, resistance, and the unwavering pursuit of liberty. His legacy serves as a constant reminder that even in the face of seemingly insurmountable odds, the human spirit's yearning for freedom can never be truly extinguished.

1833

The Slavery Abolition Act

After decades of activism, debate, and growing unrest in the colonies, the British Parliament finally passed *The Slavery Abolition Act* on August 28, 1833. This landmark legislation marked the official decision to end slavery throughout the British Empire, including Jamaica. However, while the Act was a major victory, it fell short of granting immediate and full freedom to the enslaved.

Key Provisions of the Act

Slavery was officially abolished in the British colonies; however, freedom was not immediate.

The Apprenticeship System was introduced, requiring formerly enslaved people to work unpaid for their former masters for a transitional period—until 1838 for domestic workers and 1840 for field laborers.

Planters were compensated for the loss of their enslaved labor— £20 million (a massive sum at the time, worth approximately £2.3 billion today using the Bank of England's CPI calculator) was allocated to slave owners across the empire—roughly 40% of Britain's annual budget.

Enslaved people received no compensation for their years of forced labor, nor did they receive land or resources to start independent lives.

The Role of the Baptist War

The passage of the Act was not solely the result of political or moral arguments—it was also driven by fear. The Baptist War of 1831-1832 had proven that enslaved people would no longer accept their oppression quietly. The massive rebellion in Jamaica, coupled with the long-standing efforts of abolitionists, forced the British government to act.

Abolitionists Push for More

While abolitionists celebrated the Act as a step forward, many were deeply disappointed by the inclusion of the Apprenticeship System, which they saw as an attempt to prolong slavery under another name. In the coming years, resistance to Apprenticeship would grow, leading to its early termination in 1838.

The Slavery Abolition Act of 1833 legally ended slavery in the British Empire, but freedom was not immediate. Instead, it introduced a transitional period known as the Apprenticeship System. This meant that while the legal status of slavery ended, formerly enslaved people were still required to work for their former enslavers without pay. The fight for true freedom— including land ownership, economic independence, and justice —had only just begun.

Abolition in Jamaica: Leaders Who Fought for Freedom

The battle over abolition was not just fought on plantations or in the streets of Jamaica but also in the halls of Parliament, in churches, and in the public arena. While abolitionists saw the end of slavery as a moral and humanitarian necessity, their opponents viewed it as a threat to the very foundation of the Caribbean economy and the British Empire's prosperity. The debate raged for decades, shaped by ideology, economic interests, and the undeniable reality of resistance from the enslaved people themselves.

The Case For Abolition

The abolitionist movement drew its strength from multiple fronts—religious conviction, economic change, and growing political pressure. Missionaries, social reformers, and even industrialists in Britain saw slavery as an institution that could no longer be justified.

One of the strongest arguments against slavery was rooted in morality and religion. Christian abolitionists, particularly among the Baptist, Methodist, and Moravian churches, preached that slavery was a sin against both God and humanity. Missionaries who worked directly with enslaved people in Jamaica, such as James Phillippo, saw firsthand the brutal conditions they endured. He became one of the most vocal advocates for immediate emancipation and later worked to create Free Villages, helping freed people escape planter control.

Beyond the missionaries, powerful voices in Britain fought for abolition in Parliament. William Wilberforce, the leading figure of the movement, spent decades campaigning for the end of the slave trade and, eventually, slavery itself. His passionate speeches and political lobbying led to the Slave Trade Act of 1807, but slavery in Jamaica remained intact. When he retired, Thomas Fowell Buxton took over the fight, pushing through the final abolition of slavery in 1833.

While most colonial governors sided with planters, one notable exception was Peter Browne, the Marquis of Sligo, who served as Jamaica's governor from 1834 to 1836. Unlike his predecessors,

Sligo actively supported the transition to freedom, working to ensure that the Apprenticeship System did not become another form of slavery. He encouraged land ownership among freed people and opposed planter resistance, which made him deeply unpopular with the island's elite. Sligoville, Jamaica's first Free Village, was named in his honor—symbolizing his commitment to true emancipation.

Abolitionist activists were not just politicians and missionaries— they were also on the ground in Jamaica, exposing the system's brutality. In 1837, Joseph Sturge, a Quaker abolitionist, traveled to the island to investigate the so-called Apprenticeship System. His shocking findings—of continued forced labor, whippings, and exploitation—rallied public opinion in Britain against gradualism, leading to full emancipation in 1838.

But moral and religious arguments alone weren't enough to win the fight. Economic changes in Britain were shifting the balance of power. The Industrial Revolution had moved wealth away from sugar plantations and toward manufacturing and trade. Some economists argued that free labor was actually more efficient than enslaved labor—a point reinforced by the repeated rebellions in the Caribbean.

None of these rebellions had a greater impact than the Christmas Rebellion of 1831, led by Sam Sharpe, a Baptist deacon and freedom fighter. What began as a peaceful strike escalated into a full-scale revolt, with 60,000 enslaved people rising up, setting fire to plantations, and demanding their freedom. The rebellion was brutally crushed, and Sharpe was executed in 1832—but his actions forced the British government to accept that slavery could not continue. His sacrifice directly influenced Parliament's decision to pass the 1833 Slavery Abolition Act, proving that resistance from the enslaved was just as powerful as any speech in Westminster.

These forces—moral arguments, economic shifts, and outright rebellion—coalesced into an unstoppable movement. The British public, driven by abolitionist speeches, petitions, and publications like *The Interesting Narrative of the Life of Olaudah Equiano*, pressured Parliament to act. By 1833, the momentum was too strong to ignore, and the Slavery Abolition Act was passed, marking the beginning of the end.

The Case Against Abolition

While abolitionists fought for freedom, they faced fierce resistance from powerful figures who saw slavery not as a moral question but as an economic necessity. The plantation economy of Jamaica—and the wealth it generated for Britain—depended entirely on enslaved labor. Sugar, the empire's most valuable commodity, was produced through a brutal system that had enriched generations of planters, merchants, and investors. To them, abolition was not just an attack on their profits; it was an existential threat.

One of the most influential defenders of slavery was Edward Long, a Jamaican planter and historian. His writings promoted the belief that Black people were inherently inferior, arguing that slavery was a natural and necessary institution. His racist ideology shaped public perception in Britain and provided intellectual ammunition for those seeking to delay abolition.

But the real power lay with the West India Lobby, a group of wealthy planters, traders, and merchants who controlled political influence in Britain. One of their most vocal leaders was George Hibbert, a London merchant who fought relentlessly against abolition, claiming that ending slavery would collapse Britain's economy. As a key figure in Parliament, he helped stall reforms for years, ensuring that planters could continue profiting from forced labor.

Even when abolition seemed inevitable, planters fought for gradualism. They argued that enslaved people were "not ready" for freedom, leading to the implementation of the Apprenticeship System, which forced freed people to continue working for their former masters under restrictive conditions. One of the leading voices for gradualism was John Gladstone, a plantation owner whose estates in Demerara (now Guyana) were among the most profitable in the empire. After losing the battle against slavery, he became a driving force behind indentured labor, ensuring that plantations could replace enslaved Africans with Indian and Chinese workers under new exploitative contracts.

Planters also used fear tactics, pointing to Haiti as an example of what could happen if Black people were given their freedom. Many believed that abolition would trigger mass uprisings and destroy white rule in the Caribbean. This argument was not just speculation—it was rooted in a deep fear of Black autonomy and the loss of white economic dominance.

Despite their efforts, the abolitionists ultimately won, but not without major compromises. The West India Lobby ensured that planters were compensated with £20 million (a massive sum at the time) for the loss of their "property," while freed people received nothing. Instead of immediate freedom, they endured the Apprenticeship System until 1838, keeping them under planter control for four more years.

The Legacy of the Struggle

The abolition of slavery in Jamaica was a battle of ideals, economics, and power. While abolitionists like Wilberforce, Buxton, Sturge, and Sharpe pushed for freedom, figures like Long, Hibbert, and Gladstone fought to preserve oppression.

Even after the legal end of slavery, the fight for true equality continued:

- The Apprenticeship System (1834–1838) forced freed people to keep working under harsh conditions.
- Land struggles left many Jamaicans without access to property, leading to the creation of Free Villages.
- Planters turned increasingly to indentured labor, exploiting new workers from India and China.

The struggles of that era still echo in Jamaica today—in land ownership disputes, economic inequality, and the continued fight for justice. The end of slavery was not the end of oppression. The battle over freedom did not simply conclude in 1838—it evolved into new forms of exploitation, and the legacy of that conflict is still being fought over today.

Some Key Figures in the Abolition Debate

The table that follows summarizes some of the most significant individuals on both sides of the abolition struggle. The list is not exhaustive, but these figures shaped the battle over slavery and determined the course of Jamaican history.

Abolitionists (For Emancipation)	Pro-Slavery Figures (Against Emancipation)
William Wilberforce – Led the parliamentary campaign for abolition, advocating for decades.	Edward Long – Jamaican planter and historian who promoted racist ideologies to justify slavery.
Thomas Fowell Buxton – Took over Wilberforce's fight, securing the Slavery Abolition Act of 1833.	George Hibbert – Merchant and politician who fought to protect plante interests in Parliament.
Joseph Sturge – Exposed the abuses of the Apprenticeship System, eading to full emancipation in 1838.	John Gladstone – Wealthy plantation owner who fought for gradualism and later promoted indentured labor.
James Phillippo – Baptist missionary who advocated for abolition and helped establish Free Villages.	The West India Lobby – A group of powerful plantation owners and merchants who resisted abolition.
Sam Sharpe – Led the 1831 Christma Rebellion, proving slavery was unsustainable.	Pro-Slavery Planters in Jamaica – Argued that abolition would destroy the sugar economy.
Olaudah Equiano – Former enslaved man whose autobiography fueled abolitionist sentiment.	Anti-Abolition Politicians in Parliamen – Delayed reform and secured compensation for planters.
Thomas Clarkson – Gathered evidence on the horrors of slavery, strengthening the abolitionist cause.	Pro-Slavery Writers & Newspapers – Spread fear about emancipation leading to chaos.

1834

From Slavery to Apprenticeship: The Struggle Evolves

Across Jamaica, the anticipation of freedom grew as August 1, 1834, approached. Many enslaved people fully believed that the day would bring an end to their bondage, as reports from missionaries and other observers later confirmed. But when the morning came, they discovered that slavery had not truly ended —only its name had changed.

The Apprenticeship System

Rather than granting full freedom in 1834, the British government implemented a phased approach known as the Apprenticeship system. Under this arrangement, formerly enslaved people were required to continue working for their former masters without pay for a period of four years for domestic workers and six years for field laborers. The system was justified as a way to ease the transition from slavery to a free labor economy, but in practice, it functioned as another form of forced labor and sparked widespread resentment.

- Labor requirements: Apprentices had to work 40.5 hours per week for their former owners without wages.
- Restrictions on movement: They could not leave the estates without permission.
- Brutality continued: Planters used flogging and other harsh punishments to enforce discipline.

- Economic hardship: Apprentices had to find additional work during their limited free time to earn money for food, rent, and other necessities.

From the outset, the Apprenticeship system was deeply unpopular. Many formerly enslaved people refused to accept it as true freedom, while planters resented losing full control over their labor force.

Resistance and the Fight for Full Freedom

From the moment Apprenticeship began, it was clear that true freedom had not arrived. Across Jamaica, frustration boiled over as formerly enslaved people realized they were still bound to the estates, forced to work without pay under the same brutal conditions. Many refused to accept this so-called transition and found ways to resist.

Some turned to the courts, challenging the abuses of their former masters. Others sought an escape from the system by purchasing their own freedom—but this was a cruel irony. Those who had toiled for a lifetime without wages were now expected to buy back their liberty.

To do so, they relied on any means available. Some took on additional labor during their limited free time. Others pooled resources within their families, with relatives sacrificing what little they had. Entire communities sometimes gathered funds to liberate those most vulnerable. A few were aided by missionaries, who raised money or lobbied on their behalf. But for many, the cost of freedom remained out of reach—an impossible burden for people deliberately kept in poverty.

Reports of these injustices made their way to Britain. Missionaries, who had long advocated for the rights of the enslaved, wrote letters detailing the harsh realities of

Apprenticeship. Stories of floggings, hunger, and unjust punishments outraged the British public. Many who had once celebrated abolition now felt betrayed—this was not the freedom they had envisioned.

In response to the growing outcry, Parliament launched investigations into colonial conditions. The findings were damning. The system was rife with abuse and clearly just slavery by another name. Under mounting pressure, the British government was forced to act.

The struggle for true emancipation had not ended in 1834—it had only entered a new phase. The voices of the oppressed, amplified by their allies in Britain, could not be silenced. Although Apprenticeship was originally set to continue until 1840, growing resistance in Jamaica and sustained pressure from abolitionists led to its early termination.

In 1838, just four years after its introduction, the Apprenticeship System was abolished, and full legal freedom was finally granted to all formerly enslaved people in Jamaica.

1834 - The Arrival of German Indentured Laborers

Meanwhile, as the abolition of slavery loomed in 1834, Jamaican plantation owners anticipated a labor shortage and sought alternative sources of workers. This led to the introduction of German indentured laborers, marking a significant shift in Jamaica's demographic landscape.

First Arrivals in 1834

The initial group of 64 Germans arrived in Jamaica on May 24, 1834, aboard the ship Anna. Recruited by Solomon Myers, a German-Jewish plantation owner, they were settled on his coffee plantation, Mount Pleasant, in the mountains above Buff Bay. These early arrivals included skilled workers such as weavers, tailors, coppersmiths, and ploughmen.

Later that year, in December 1834, Myers facilitated the arrival of an additional 506 Germans aboard the ship Olbers. Unlike the first group, these new arrivals were dispersed across several plantations under British planters:

- St. George (now Portland): 20 individuals remained with Myers.
- St. Ann's Bay: 150 individuals placed under Hamilton Brown.
- Dry Harbour Mountains, St. Ann: 45 individuals assigned to James Hylton's estate.
- Montego Bay: 20 individuals placed with Samuel Anderson.
- Black River & Lacovia, St. Elizabeth: 150 individuals sent to Robert Watt's estates, with 102 in Lacovia.
- Clarendon & Manchester: 120 individuals assigned to Dr. Spaulding and another plantation owner.

This strategy of dispersing European immigrants was part of a broader colonial initiative to integrate non-African laborers into the workforce, though many of these laborers struggled to adapt to Jamaica's conditions. Many were unprepared for the Caribbean climate, suffered from tropical diseases, and lacked experience with plantation work, making survival difficult.

1835

Sligoville and the Birth of Free Villages

In 1835, Sligoville became the first Free Village in Jamaica, marking a pivotal moment in the transition from slavery to freedom. The village was established by Baptist missionary James Mursell Phillippo, who purchased 25 acres of land using funds from the Baptist Missionary Society and other British abolitionist networks. His goal was to create a self-sufficient settlement for formerly enslaved individuals. Sligoville was named in honor of Howe Peter Browne, 2nd Marquess of Sligo, the Governor of Jamaica, who supported emancipation efforts.

This initiative laid the groundwork for similar villages across the island, providing a crucial alternative to the plantation system.

A Sanctuary from Apprenticeship

At the time, most of Jamaica's formerly enslaved population was still bound by the apprenticeship system, which required them to continue working for their former enslavers under restrictive conditions. Sligoville offered an escape from this structure, allowing settlers to begin building independent lives away from direct plantation control. While some settlers may have been manumitted or had purchased their freedom before full emancipation, the majority were apprentices seeking refuge from the lingering grip of the plantation economy.

Establishing a New Way of Life

The land in Sligoville was divided into plots where settlers could construct homes, cultivate crops, and establish small businesses. The village also became a center for education and religious instruction, with churches and schools playing a central role in community development. Phillippo and other missionaries saw Free Villages as not only a path to economic independence but also a means of instilling Christian values and fostering social stability.

The Legacy of Sligoville

Sligoville set the precedent for a wave of Free Villages across Jamaica, demonstrating that formerly enslaved people could build thriving communities outside the control of the plantation system. Its success challenged the fears of plantation owners who believed that freed people would be unable to sustain themselves independently. By the time full emancipation arrived in 1838, Sligoville had already proven the potential for a new society based on self-sufficiency and communal resilience.

Sligoville remains a historic symbol of resistance and progress, marking the first step toward true freedom for Jamaica's formerly enslaved population.

1835 - The Establishment of Seaford Town

While Sligoville represented a step toward emancipation and self-reliance, the colonial government pursued a separate goal in 1835: the encouragement of European immigration. This policy, known as Bountied European Immigration, was intended to supplement the labor force and populate Jamaica's interior with European settlers to reinforce colonial control.

A significant outcome of this policy was the creation of Seaford Town, a German settlement located in Westmoreland. The initiative was led by Lord Seaford (Charles Ellis, 1st Baron Seaford), who donated 500 acres of his Montpelier estate for the establishment of a permanent German community. Unlike the Free Villages, which were built for freed Jamaicans, Seaford Town was designed specifically for German indentured laborers and settlers.

Challenges and Adaptation

The settlers of Seaford Town faced numerous difficulties in their early years. Many were unprepared for Jamaica's tropical climate and challenging farming conditions. Disease, isolation, and economic hardship took their toll, leading some settlers to abandon the town, while others integrated into neighboring Jamaican communities. Despite these setbacks, Seaford Town persisted, evolving into a distinct cultural enclave.

Cultural Contributions and Legacy

- Agriculture: German settlers introduced European farming techniques that influenced local agricultural practices.
- Architecture: They constructed European-style homes, some featuring basements uncommon in Jamaica.
- Surnames and Identity: Although the German language eventually faded, surnames like Zink, Stolz, and Höfele remain common in the region.

Seaford Town continues to stand as a reminder of Jamaica's diverse cultural history. Its descendants maintain German-Jamaican traditions, preserve historic buildings, and celebrate the cultural heritage passed down through generations.

Sligoville and Seaford Town: Understanding the Distinction

While both Sligoville and Seaford Town were established in 1835, their purposes were fundamentally different.

- **Sligoville** was the first Free Village specifically created to provide land and housing for freed Jamaicans. Established by Baptist missionaries like Phillippo, it served as a refuge for those escaping the restrictions of the apprenticeship system.
- **Seaford Town** was part of the colonial government's effort to settle European immigrants. Unlike Free Villages, it was not intended to support the formerly enslaved but to bolster the European population in Jamaica.

Significance to Emancipation

- **Sligoville** directly supported the transition from slavery to freedom by offering a sustainable, independent future for formerly enslaved people.
- **Seaford Town** was not established to support formerly enslaved people, but rather as part of a colonial effort to settle European laborers in Jamaica following emancipation.

Legacy and Recognition

- **Sligoville** remains a symbol of resistance and resilience, representing the success of the Free Village movement in helping freed people gain land and independence.
- **Seaford Town** reflects the legacy of German-Jamaican heritage and stands as a reminder of the complexities of Jamaica's colonial past.

By understanding the distinct purposes of these two settlements, we gain deeper insight into the diverse forces that shaped Jamaica's post-emancipation society.

The Rise of Free Villages Across Jamaica

While Sligoville was the first Free Village and a pioneering symbol of Black autonomy, it was just the beginning. The concept of Free Villages quickly spread across Jamaica as missionaries, abolitionists, and freed people collaborated to create settlements where formerly enslaved individuals could live independently of the plantation system. This movement represented a direct challenge to planter dominance and reshaped the island's social and economic landscape. The following section explores the growth of Free Villages, the obstacles their residents faced, and the legacy they left behind.

The Weight of Freedom: Charting Your Own Course

The abolition of slavery in Jamaica in 1838 marked the beginning of a new chapter for formerly enslaved people. But with freedom came uncertainty and challenge. Many freed Jamaicans found themselves economically disadvantaged, lacking land, resources, and opportunities to build independent lives. In response, the Free Villages movement evolved—self-sustaining communities where freed individuals could live free from planter control and develop economic independence.

These villages, founded primarily by the Baptist, Methodist, and Moravian missionaries, played a crucial role in shaping post-emancipation Jamaican society. They laid the foundation for the emerging peasant economy, fostered autonomy, and strengthened Jamaica's cultural and social identity. The movement also met fierce resistance from plantation owners, who sought to keep freed people dependent on estate labor.

The Birth of Free Villages: Sligoville and Beyond

In 1835, Baptist missionary James Mursell Phillippo facilitated the establishment of Sligoville, the first Free Village in Jamaica. Named in honor of Howe Peter Browne, the 2nd Marquess of Sligo, who served as Governor of Jamaica from 1834 to 1836 and supported emancipation efforts, Sligoville provided an alternative to the plantation system at a time when most formerly enslaved people were still bound by the Apprenticeship System—a transitional arrangement meant to phase out slavery but which largely kept planters in control of labor.

For many apprentices, Free Villages offered a rare chance to escape the oppressive conditions of plantation life. Some settlers had been manumitted before full emancipation, while others saved their meager wages to buy their freedom. However, the majority of Free Village settlers were still apprentices who sought to secure land and establish homes in these villages before the mandatory end of apprenticeship in 1838, even though they were still legally bound to plantation labor.

Phillippo and other missionaries saw Free Villages as more than just settlements—they were intended to be self-sufficient communities with land ownership, churches, schools, and economic opportunities. The success of Sligoville soon inspired similar settlements across Jamaica, laying the groundwork for a widespread movement.

How Free Villages Operated

Unlike the plantation system, which kept laborers tied to estates without property rights, Free Villages allowed formerly enslaved individuals to own land—a transformative shift that challenged planter dominance.

Land Ownership and Economic Independence

Villagers were required to purchase plots of land, often with assistance from missionary societies. Prices varied, and while some freed individuals managed to buy land outright, others struggled to afford it due to high costs and limited access to credit. Missionary groups sometimes helped by securing land at reduced rates or offering payment plans.

Once settled, villagers cultivated small farms, growing food crops such as yam, cassava, and plantains alongside cash crops like coffee and pimento. This shift laid the foundation for Jamaica's peasant farming economy, reducing reliance on plantation labor and increasing economic self-sufficiency.

Religious and Educational Centers

Churches and schools were central to Free Village life. Baptist, Methodist, and Moravian missionaries saw these institutions as essential for spiritual and social development. Schools provided basic education, equipping children with literacy and numeracy skills that had been denied to enslaved populations. Churches reinforced Christian teachings while also serving as community hubs for meetings, dispute resolution, and resistance to planter influence.

Resistance from Plantation Owners

Many planters viewed Free Villages as a direct threat to their control. Planters had expected freed people to remain as wage laborers on estates. The rise of independent communities not only disrupted the labor supply but also threatened their economic and social dominance. In response, planters employed various tactics to undermine Free Villages:

- Restricting Land Sales — Some plantation owners refused to sell land to freed people, forcing missionaries to purchase plots on their behalf.
- Economic Pressure — Planters restricted access to markets and controlled trade networks to keep freed people financially dependent.
- Legal Barriers — Planters lobbied for restrictions on land access and used their influence to discourage sales to freed people.
- Violence and Intimidation — Freed villagers often faced threats, attacks, or arson from planters and their supporters, who resented their growing independence.

Despite these challenges, the Free Village movement expanded, demonstrating the resilience and determination of Jamaica's freed population.

Key Free Villages and Their Founders

Following Sligoville, numerous Free Villages emerged across Jamaica. Some of the most notable include:

- Sturge Town (St. Ann) – 1839: Founded by Baptist missionaries and named after British abolitionist Joseph Sturge.
- Buxton (St. Ann) – 1840: Established by Moravian missionaries and named after abolitionist Thomas Fowell Buxton.
- Kitson Town (St. Catherine) – 1840s: Developed with the help of free Black Jamaicans to provide land access to freed individuals.
- Bethel Town (Westmoreland) – 1838: A Methodist-founded village that became a center for small-scale farming.

- Mount Industry (St. Catherine) – 1838: Another Baptist-founded Free Village, promoting land ownership and economic self-reliance.

Key Figures Behind Free Villages

- James Phillippo: Baptist missionary and founder of Sligoville.
- Joseph Sturge: British Quaker abolitionist who funded Sturge Town and advocated for land rights.
- Thomas Fowell Buxton: British MP who led abolitionist efforts and supported Free Villages.
- Howe Peter Browne, the 2nd Marquess of Sligo: Governor of Jamaica who pushed for fairer treatment of freed people, after whom the first village was named.

Legacy of the Free Villages

The Free Village movement transformed post-emancipation Jamaica, enabling freed people to own land, build communities, and resist planter control.

These settlements:

- Provided a path to economic independence through land ownership and small farming.
- Established churches and schools that strengthened Black social and political identity.
- Laid the foundation for Jamaica's peasant economy, which persisted well into the 20th century.
- Fostered a sense of self-governance and resistance that influenced later struggles for land rights and political representation.

Many Free Villages still exist today, standing as enduring symbols of resilience, freedom, and the pursuit of self-determination.

Conclusion

The Free Village movement was a radical response to the failures of emancipation, offering Jamaica's formerly enslaved population the opportunity to reclaim their autonomy. Despite intense opposition from planters, these communities flourished, proving that freed people could build thriving, self-sustaining settlements. Through land ownership, education, and religious leadership, the Free Villages played a crucial role in shaping Jamaica's post-slavery society.

1838

Emancipation Day — The End of Slavery and Apprenticeship

On August 1, 1838, the dawn of freedom broke across Jamaica as the island witnessed one of the most significant moments in its history—the complete abolition of slavery and the end of the Apprenticeship System. After centuries of forced labor and oppression, 311,000 formerly enslaved people finally gained full legal freedom. Across the island, churches overflowed, bells rang, and hymns of liberation echoed through towns and villages as freed people celebrated their long-awaited emancipation.

A Historic Celebration in Spanish Town

One of the largest and most documented celebrations took place in Spanish Town, the capital of colonial Jamaica. Under the leadership of Reverend James Mursell Phillippo, the Baptist Church congregation organized a grand procession to Government House, where they would be received by Governor Sir Lionel Smith.

The procession included around 2,000 children from Baptist mission schools, along with their teachers and thousands of freed people, all marching in celebration. By the time they reached Government House, around 8,000 people had gathered with great anticipation to witness the formal declaration of freedom.

Governor Smith addressed the crowd, acknowledging the significance of the moment, then read the Proclamation of Freedom. Cheers erupted as people wept with joy, prayed, and sang hymns—a powerful expression of the faith and resilience that had carried them through generations of enslavement.

As a symbol of unity, Governor Smith, Reverend Phillippo, and the Bishop of Jamaica stood together on the front portico of Government House, representing the collaboration between civil and religious efforts that helped bring about emancipation.

After the reading of the Proclamation of Freedom, the massive gathering peacefully dispersed, with families returning to their homes to reflect on their newfound liberty.

Island-Wide Celebrations

The joy of emancipation was not confined to Spanish Town. Throughout Jamaica's parishes, similar celebrations took place, demonstrating the depth of emotion and the overwhelming sense of liberation that the day carried.

- Churches held all-night services on July 31, leading into special worship sessions on August 1.
- Bells rang out, and hymns of freedom filled the air as thousands gathered in town centers and villages.
- Public processions and feasts were organized in multiple parishes, with freed people dressing in their finest clothing to mark the day with dignity and celebration.
- Missionary leaders emphasized education and land ownership, encouraging freed individuals to focus on building sustainable communities and securing their independence.
- Former apprentices, now truly free, openly rejected returning to plantation work, sparking the beginnings of Jamaica's peasant economy.

While August 1, 1838, marked the legal end of slavery, the struggle for economic and social freedom was far from over. However, the day became an enduring symbol of resilience, hope, and self-determination.

Emancipation Day as a Public Holiday

For many years, the legacy of August 1 was commemorated through church services, processions, and local celebrations. In 1893, Emancipation Day was first recognized as a public holiday in Jamaica. However, in 1962, following Jamaica's independence, the holiday was discontinued and replaced by Independence Day, observed on August 6.

A movement to reinstate Emancipation Day as a national holiday gained momentum in the 1990s, led by figures such as Professor Rex Nettleford. In 1997, under the administration of

Prime Minister P.J. Patterson, Emancipation Day was reinstated as a national public holiday, observed annually on August 1.

Today, Emancipation Day is a time of reflection, cultural pride, and remembrance, honoring the sacrifices and perseverance of those who fought for freedom.

Emancipation Celebrations Across Jamaica's Parishes

St. Catherine (Spanish Town) – The Official Proclamation

- The most well-documented celebration took place in Spanish Town, then the capital of Jamaica.
- A massive procession led by the Baptist Church and congregation, with around 2,000 children from Baptist schools, teachers, and freed people.
- Governor Smith read the Proclamation of Freedom to an estimated 8,000 people, followed by prayers and hymns.
- The crowd peacefully dispersed after the ceremony.

Kingston – Churches Overflowing with Worshippers

- Churches were filled to overflowing as people gathered for prayers.
- The ringing of church bells at dawn signaled the arrival of full freedom.
- Hymns of liberation were sung throughout the streets.

St. James (Montego Bay) – A Coastal Celebration

- A large crowd assembled in the town center to listen to the reading of the Proclamation.
- Freed people sang hymns and marched through Montego Bay's streets.

Trelawny (Falmouth) – Processions and Public Readings

- Freed people gathered in Falmouth Square to witness a public reading of the Proclamation.
- Church bells rang out in celebration.

Westmoreland – Midnight Prayers and Morning Celebrations

- Churches in Savanna-la-Mar were filled for overnight prayers.
- Missionaries held sunrise services, marking the transition to freedom.

Clarendon – Plantation Tensions and Public Gatherings

- Religious services were held across May Pen and neighboring settlements.
- Freed people who had been saving wages made plans to purchase land in upcoming Free Village developments.

Conclusion

Emancipation Day, August 1, 1838, marked not only the legal end of slavery in Jamaica but also the beginning of a new struggle—one for land, opportunity, and dignity. While true freedom would take generations to fully realize, the celebrations that swept across the island on that historic day were a powerful declaration: the people of Jamaica would never again live in bondage. Their hope, faith, and determination laid the foundation for a nation still rising from the ashes of enslavement.

1844

The Beginning of Jamaica's Railway System

In 1844, the Railway Company of Jamaica was established, launching the first major railway construction project in the British Caribbean. The initiative was led by William and David Smith, both brothers and British investors with landholdings in Jamaica. Although the colonial government granted them a franchise to build and operate the railway, the project was primarily privately funded and managed, with some indirect government support.

The railway was conceived primarily to support the struggling sugar industry, which had been facing labor shortages and rising costs following the abolition of slavery. Planters needed an efficient means of transporting sugar and rum from estates to Kingston's port, as reliance on carts and mule-drawn wagons over Jamaica's poor roads was slow, costly, and unreliable. The railway promised greater efficiency and reduced transportation costs, making sugar exports more competitive in an era of increasing global competition.

Beyond its immediate role in serving the plantation economy, the railway represented an important step toward modernizing Jamaica's infrastructure. Improved transportation had the potential to stimulate internal trade, linking Kingston with inland settlements and facilitating commerce between growing towns. While sugar remained dominant in 1844, the railway's construction set the stage for future expansions that would later support Jamaica's emerging peasant economy and the transport of other goods, including coffee and bananas.

The establishment of the railway was not merely a lifeline for plantations—it was a turning point in Jamaica's commercial development, laying the foundation for an integrated transport network that would shape the island's economy for generations to come.

1845

Jamaica Opens Its First Railway Line

On November 21, 1845, Jamaica became the second British colony, after Canada, to open and operate a railway system. The first line, stretching 14.5 miles from Kingston to Angels (near Spanish Town), was privately constructed and operated by the Railway Company of Jamaica, founded by William and David Smith.

Originally built to serve the sugar industry, the railway provided planters with a faster, more efficient means of transporting cane to coastal ports. However, as Jamaica's peasant economy expanded, its influence reached far beyond the plantations. The improved transportation network stimulated internal trade, making it easier to move goods between Kingston and inland agricultural regions. For small farmers and merchants, the railway became a vital lifeline, opening access to broader markets and creating new economic opportunities that reshaped the island's commercial landscape.

The success of this first railway line marked the beginning of a new era in Jamaican infrastructure. Though its early development was closely tied to the plantation economy, the railway would eventually play a pivotal role in Jamaica's economic diversification, supporting industries such as bananas, coffee, and commerce. Over time, the expansion of the railway would transform the island's connectivity, linking rural communities to urban centers and helping to shape Jamaica's modern economy.

Also in 1845: The Arrival of Indian Indentured Workers

While the railway was changing Jamaica's physical landscape, another major transformation was beginning in its labor force and demographic makeup. On May 10, 1845, the first East Indian indentured workers arrived, mostly from Uttar Pradesh and Bihar. Their arrival marked the start of a massive migration wave, with over 36,000 Indians coming to Jamaica between 1845 and 1917, primarily to work on sugar plantations.

Like their African predecessors, many Indian laborers faced harsh conditions and longed for greater economic freedom. Over time, many left plantation life to establish small businesses, particularly in retail and agriculture. Their cultural influence remains deeply woven into Jamaican society, shaping key aspects of daily life, language, and cuisine:

- Cuisine: The introduction of curry dishes, roti, and dhal, now staples of Jamaican cooking.
- Language: Hindi words like chutney and jahaji (shipmate) became part of Jamaican Patois.
- Religion: Hindu and Muslim traditions influenced Jamaican spirituality, though many later converted to Christianity.

The year 1845 was a turning point in Jamaica's history—not only did it usher in a new era of transportation and commerce, but it also laid the foundation for one of the most significant cultural shifts in the island's identity.

1846

The Sugar Duties Act & Economic Collapse

By the mid-19th century, Britain was moving toward free trade, abandoning the economic protections that had long benefited its Caribbean colonies. This shift would prove disastrous for Jamaica's sugar industry.

The end of slavery had already weakened the plantation economy, but Jamaica's sugar industry collapsed completely in 1846 when the British government passed the Sugar Duties Act, which removed preferential tariffs for British Caribbean sugar. This allowed cheaper, slave-produced sugar from Cuba and Brazil to dominate the market, devastating Jamaican exports.

Sugar from Cuba and Brazil, where slavery was still legal, flooded the market at lower prices, leaving Jamaican planters unable to compete. Within years, many estates were abandoned, and the economic power of the plantocracy—the ruling class of sugar planters—began to fade. Some planters left the island altogether, with several migrating to British Honduras (Belize), Trinidad, and even Cuba in search of more profitable conditions. Others, determined to sustain their estates, turned to indentured labor, importing workers from India and China to replace the freed population, who had largely refused to return to plantation labor under exploitative conditions.

Yet, as the estates withered, a new economy was quietly taking shape. Freed Jamaicans turned to independent farming, cultivating food crops and small provisions for themselves. Though they struggled under British policies that restricted land ownership, they were laying the foundation for Jamaica's peasant economy, a system that would outlast the dying plantation model.

1854

Arrival of Chinese Indentured Workers

The first group of 224 Chinese indentured laborers arrived in Jamaica in 1854, part of a broader effort by colonial authorities to replace emancipated African labor with indentured workers from Asia. The newcomers were recruited primarily from southern China and were initially contracted to work on sugar plantations under harsh and unfamiliar conditions.

The first group of Chinese immigrants arrived in Jamaica from Hong Kong aboard the Epsom on July 30, 1854. Later that year, a second group of 197 Chinese laborers arrived aboard the Vampire in November. These individuals were part of a larger group of over 1,000 originally contracted to work on the Panama Railroad. However, a deadly yellow fever outbreak in Panama halted progress and prompted authorities there to relocate surplus laborers. With Jamaica actively seeking additional workers for its plantation economy, the colonial government agreed to receive a portion of these redirected Chinese immigrants.

Subsequent waves of Chinese migrants arrived in 1870, 1884, and 1891, with more continuing into the early 20th century. While many Chinese indentured workers struggled on the plantations, a large number eventually left estate labor behind, turning instead to commerce and trade.

Over time, Chinese Jamaicans became deeply embedded in the island's economic and cultural landscape. Known for their entrepreneurial spirit, many opened grocery shops, bakeries, and restaurants. Their small corner shops, or "Chinese shops," became fixtures in communities across the island, offering essential goods often on credit—a practice known as selling on "trust." They also popularized the custom of giving a "brawta," a little extra added to a purchase as a gesture of goodwill, which endeared them to many customers and helped entrench their role in the retail trade.

Their contributions touched nearly every aspect of Jamaican life, including:

- Cuisine: Fried rice, Chinese pastries, sweet-and-sour dishes, and soy-based ingredients became woven into Jamaican culinary culture.
- Business and Trade: Chinese Jamaicans helped shape the island's retail and wholesale sectors, becoming influential figures in commerce and entrepreneurship.
- Language and Identity: Surnames such as Chin, Lee, Wong, and Chang remain common today. Elements of Cantonese and Hakka language have left subtle influences on Jamaican Patois.
- Community Legacy: Despite facing discrimination, the Chinese community maintained strong cultural traditions while integrating into wider Jamaican society. They

played a vital role in the development of the island's middle class.

By the early 20th century, the Chinese Jamaican presence had evolved from indentured roots to a vibrant and resilient community, leaving a lasting legacy in business, culture, and national identity.

1860

Coconut: The Island's Versatile Export

By the 1860s, coconuts had become one of Jamaica's most versatile exports. Originally introduced by Spanish settlers, the coconut palm thrived in Jamaica's coastal regions, particularly in St. Thomas, Portland, St. Mary and Westmoreland.

Unlike sugar or coffee, coconuts were a low-maintenance crop, providing copra (dried coconut meat), coconut oil, and fiber for domestic use and export. The oil, extracted from dried coconut meat, was used in cooking, cosmetics, and soap production, making it a highly valuable commodity in Britain, the United States, and Canada.

By 1890, Jamaica was a leading supplier of coconut oil and copra, but the industry suffered setbacks due to hurricanes, disease, and market shifts. The spread of lethal yellowing disease in the 20th century devastated many plantations, causing a sharp decline in production. Despite this, coconuts remain an important part of Jamaica's agricultural economy, with coconut water, oil, and related products still widely produced.

1865

The Morant Bay Rebellion

Three decades after emancipation, freed Jamaicans remained trapped in poverty, their dreams of land ownership and political equality blocked by the colonial system. The white planter class, though economically weakened, still dominated the island's political structure, enforcing high poll taxes, harsh legal policies, and exploitative labor conditions on the Black majority.

The Morant Bay Rebellion, which erupted on October 11, 1865, in southeastern Jamaica, was rooted in these systemic injustices. Freedmen were disenfranchised by poll taxes—voting was conditional on tax payment—which, while modest in absolute terms, were unaffordable for many Black Jamaicans, effectively excluding them from the political process.

A series of crop failures—caused by floods, droughts, and outbreaks of cholera and smallpox—further deepened rural hardship. Meanwhile, land ownership remained elusive for most freed Jamaicans, stifling economic independence and fueling discontent.

Paul Bogle, a Baptist deacon from the village of Stony Gut, emerged as a leading voice for justice and reform. His church served not only as a place of worship but also as a space for political education and resistance. Bogle drew from both Christian teachings and real-life hardship to challenge the inequities of post-emancipation Jamaica. In August 1865, he walked nearly 45 miles to Spanish Town to present grievances to Governor Edward Eyre but was refused an audience.

The Rebellion

Tensions escalated on October 7, when a man connected to Bogle's circle protested during a local trial and was arrested, sparking a confrontation with police. When warrants were issued for Bogle and his followers, it pushed an already volatile situation to the brink.

On October 11, Bogle led several hundred supporters on a march from Stony Gut to the courthouse in Morant Bay. Armed mostly with sticks and machetes, they sought justice during a vestry meeting. Expecting unrest, local authorities had assembled a volunteer militia. When stones were thrown at the militia, the soldiers opened fire, killing seven. Enraged, the crowd retaliated —burning the courthouse and surrounding buildings. Several local officials died in the melee.

For two days, the "rebels"—protesters turned insurgents—held sway in parts of St. Thomas-in-the-East parish. They raided police stations for weapons, attacked plantations, and demanded justice in the absence of legal recourse. In total, 25 people were killed during the initial clashes.

Colonial Response

Governor Eyre declared martial law in the parish and dispatched troops under Brigadier-General Alexander Nelson to suppress the rebellion. Among those enlisted to assist were the Maroons, whose participation was a byproduct of the agreement reached over a century earlier when they signed peace treaties with the British in 1739. Under those treaties, the Maroons were obligated to help suppress rebellions. Historically, they had also assisted in quelling earlier uprisings, including Tacky's War in

1760 and the Baptist War of 1831 led by Sam Sharpe—highlighting the complex and often controversial nature of their role in colonial Jamaica.

The suppression was swift and brutal:

- Over 400 people were killed, many without trial.
- More than 600 were flogged or imprisoned.
- Villages such as Stony Gut were destroyed, leaving families homeless.

Paul Bogle was captured on October 22, reportedly betrayed by local informants. He was tried under martial law and executed two days later alongside fourteen others, including his brother Moses. George William Gordon—a mixed-race legislator, landowner, and vocal critic of Eyre—was arrested in Kingston (outside the area under martial law), transferred to Morant Bay, and executed on October 23 after a rushed trial that lacked credible evidence. His execution, like Bogle's, would later spark widespread outrage.

George William Gordon had long been a thorn in the side of Governor Eyre. As a member of the Jamaican Assembly and a staunch advocate for the rights of the Black majority, Gordon publicly condemned the injustices of the colonial system and supported Bogle's calls for peaceful protest. Though he had no direct involvement in the uprising, Eyre viewed him as a dangerous agitator. His arrest in Kingston—well outside the martial law zone—was widely seen as a political move. After being transported to Morant Bay, Gordon was hastily tried by a military tribunal and sentenced to death. His execution, carried out just one day after Bogle's, outraged abolitionists and reformers in Britain and ultimately led to a Royal Commission of Inquiry and calls for Eyre to be held accountable.

Aftermath and Legacy

The Morant Bay Rebellion became one of the most infamous instances of colonial violence in the British West Indies. In total, 439 people were killed during or after the rebellion, and hundreds more were imprisoned, flogged, or subjected to forced labor.

The response divided British public opinion. While some—including conservative colonial officials—praised Governor Eyre for maintaining order, others condemned his actions as brutal and unlawful. Leading British intellectuals such as philosopher John Stuart Mill and scientist Charles Darwin joined the outcry against Eyre. Mill helped form the Jamaica Committee, which pushed for Eyre's prosecution for murder and abuse of power. Although a Royal Commission of Inquiry criticized Eyre's handling of the crisis, he was never formally charged.

The rebellion's political consequences were profound. In 1866, Britain dissolved Jamaica's local Assembly and imposed direct Crown Colony rule—ending planter dominance but centralizing power in the hands of British officials, with little immediate improvement for the Black majority.

Yet what followed was equally remarkable: the events in Jamaica ignited an unprecedented debate in Britain about imperial justice. A group known as the Jamaica Committee, led by thinkers such as John Stuart Mill, Charles Darwin, Herbert Spencer, and Thomas Huxley, sought to prosecute Governor Eyre for murder and abuse of power. Darwin—best known for his theory of evolution—had no direct connection to Jamaica but supported the Committee because he believed Eyre had violated the law, and that British justice must apply equally across the empire.

Opposing them was the Eyre Defence Committee, formed to defend Eyre's actions and legacy. Its members included the famous writer Charles Dickens, historian Thomas Carlyle, and art critic John Ruskin. These influential figures feared that holding Eyre accountable would undermine colonial authority and embolden resistance across the empire. Dickens, famed for A Tale of Two Cities and Oliver Twist, argued that strong measures were necessary to preserve order in the colonies.

That a rebellion on a small Caribbean island could divide some of Britain's greatest minds reveals the global significance of the Morant Bay Rebellion. The names Darwin and Dickens—so often associated with science and literature—stood on opposite sides of a moral and political reckoning rooted in Jamaican soil.

National Heroes Declared

Paul Bogle and George William Gordon were later declared National Heroes of Jamaica for their courageous stand for justice, land reform, and civil rights. Their legacy remains a powerful symbol of the long struggle for true emancipation.

Part 6

1866 – 1938: Colonial Reform and the Road to Nationalism

As a Crown Colony, the Governor—appointed by the Crown —now ruled without a locally elected legislature. The British Colonial Office in London had direct control over policy and governance. Local laws were made by an appointed council, not elected representatives. Under the previous structure, the Governor was also appointed by the Crown but shared power with a local Assembly—elected by a small, mostly white, property-owning electorate—and a Legislative Council, which served as an appointed advisory upper house.

After Jamaica became a Crown Colony in 1866, British authorities introduced reforms aimed at stabilizing governance and revitalizing the economy. The late 19th and early 20th centuries were marked by infrastructural growth, the expansion of peasant farming, and the growing influence of immigrant communities—particularly Indians and Chinese. However, deep-rooted racial and economic inequalities persisted, fueling growing demands for political representation and workers' rights. The labor uprisings of 1938 marked the beginning of modern political movements, giving rise to the leaders who would eventually guide Jamaica toward self-governance.

1866

The End of Planter Rule & the Birth of Crown Colony Government

The brutality of Governor Edward Eyre's suppression of the Morant Bay Rebellion shocked Britain's political establishment. The scale of the reprisals exposed the failures of Jamaica's planter-led government, proving that the white oligarchy could no longer effectively rule the colony.

In 1866, Britain dissolved Jamaica's Assembly, stripping the local elite of power and placing the island under direct rule from London. Jamaica was now a Crown Colony, meaning:

- "The British governor had full executive power, making final decisions on laws, policies, and governance."

- The old plantocracy lost its grip on political control, though many planters remained influential in economic affairs.

- Local representation was severely limited, with Jamaicans having even less political power than before.

While Crown Colony rule weakened the old plantocracy, it also meant that Jamaicans now had to appeal directly to Britain for political change, delaying real self-government for decades.

The Morant Bay Rebellion had forced Britain's hand, proving that the old colonial order was unsustainable. Though freedom had been won in 1838, true political rights and land access remained out of reach. The fight for self-governance was far from over.

1870

The Rise of the Peasant Economy & the Birth of Jamaica's Banana Industry

With sugar in decline, Jamaica's economic structure began shifting toward small-scale farming. Though still facing discrimination and legal obstacles, many freed Jamaicans purchased land, formed self-sufficient communities, and cultivated cash crops like bananas, coffee, and pimento. This shift laid the foundation for Jamaica's peasant farming economy, which would sustain rural communities for generations to come.

One of the most transformative developments in this period was the birth of Jamaica's banana industry. While bananas had been grown locally for some time, it was Lorenzo Dow Baker, an American sea captain and entrepreneur, who saw their potential as a major export crop.

Lorenzo Dow Baker & the Birth of the Banana Trade

In 1870, Lorenzo Dow Baker sailed into Port Antonio, Jamaica, where he purchased bananas from local farmers and transported them to Boston, Massachusetts. The fruit sold quickly, fetching significantly higher prices than in Jamaica, and Baker realized he had discovered a highly profitable trade opportunity.

Recognizing the demand for bananas in the United States, Baker established a direct trade route between Jamaica and the U.S., ensuring regular shipments of bananas to northern markets. His success led to the founding of the Boston Fruit Company, which later merged into what would become the United Fruit Company (UFC)—a corporation that would go on to dominate Jamaica's banana trade for decades.

By the 1870s, Jamaican farmers were exporting bananas to the U.S. and Britain, benefiting from new shipping routes and growing consumer demand. The colonial government, recognizing the economic potential, invested in infrastructure to support small farmers.

By the 1890s, banana cultivation had surpassed sugar as Jamaica's leading agricultural export, reshaping rural economies and shifting labor away from sugar plantations and toward smallholder banana cultivation.

Infrastructure & Expansion of the Banana Economy

To ensure the efficient transport of bananas, investments were made in roads, shipping ports, and later, the railway system. By 1894, the railway was expanded, linking Kingston with the interior, making it easier for rural farmers to transport their produce to market. The banana trade offered a lifeline to Jamaica's small farmers, many of whom had struggled for decades under an economic system still heavily tilted in favor of large landowners.

However, as the banana industry flourished, corporate interests tightened their grip. The United Fruit Company, now the dominant force in the trade, controlled distribution, shipping, and pricing, leaving many small Jamaican farmers struggling to compete. While some farmers prospered, many were squeezed out by the United Fruit Company's monopolistic practices, reinforcing longstanding economic disparities.

Despite these challenges, the peasant farming economy had firmly taken root—one that would sustain rural Jamaicans long after sugar's collapse. The rise of bananas as a major export crop turned Port Antonio into a key hub of international trade, anchoring Jamaica's economy more deeply into global markets. While small farmers fought to secure their share of this prosperity, large corporations like the United Fruit Company continued to dominate the industry.

The Rise of Port Antonio

The growth of the Banana Trade also played a major role in transforming Port Antonio from a quiet coastal town into one of the island's first tourist destinations. Profits from the Boston Fruit Company allowed Baker to invest heavily in the town's infrastructure financing roads, a wharf, and warehouse facilities to support both the banana trade and the growing interest in tourism.

In the late 1890s, leveraging the success of his ventures, Baker built the Titchfield Hotel on the Titchfield Peninsula overlooking the harbor. It became one of the Caribbean's most luxurious hotels and was instrumental in attracting wealthy North American tourists to Jamaica. The hotel was one of the first in Jamaica to offer modern amenities, and it helped establish the idea of Jamaica as a tropical escape.

The Rise of Banana Tourism

Baker and the Boston Fruit Company made Port Antonio the hub of banana exports. As steamships regularly docked to collect fruit, the same vessels began carrying wealthy American tourists. This banana-tourism dual economy made Port Antonio a unique case in Jamaica—combining agriculture, commerce, and early tourism development. This blend of agriculture and tourism in Port Antonio foreshadowed Jamaica's dual identity in the 20th century—as both a breadbasket and a tourist paradise.

1872

Kingston Becomes the Capital of Jamaica

For over three centuries, Spanish Town (formerly St. Jago de la Vega) had served as Jamaica's administrative capital. However, by the late 19th century, Kingston had grown into the island's commercial and cultural hub, surpassing Spanish Town in economic significance and infrastructure.

Several factors influenced the decision to relocate the capital:

- **Port Accessibility:** Kingston's natural harbor was one of the best in the Caribbean, making it the center of trade and commerce.
- **Economic Growth:** Kingston had developed rapidly, with new businesses, banks, and institutions forming the backbone of Jamaica's economy.
- **Urban Development:** The rebuilding efforts after the 1692 earthquake, the 1703 fire, and ongoing expansions made Kingston the island's most modern city.

- **Spanish Town's Decline:** The old capital was losing prominence as Kingston became the focal point of Jamaica's economy and society.

In 1872, the colonial government formally transferred the capital from Spanish Town to Kingston. Government offices, the governor's residence, and key institutions were moved to the city, solidifying Kingston's status as Jamaica's political and economic center.

Today, Kingston remains the heart of Jamaica, home to its government, cultural institutions, and thriving industries.

1876

Jamaica's Tramcar System: From Horse-Drawn to Electric

Urban transportation in Jamaica took a major leap forward in the 1870s when Kingston's population growth demanded more efficient means of mobility. In 1876, the Jamaica Street Car Company was formed by American engineer Tracy Robinson— who had previously worked on the Panama Railway project— and local businessman Samuel Constantine Burke, who secured a concession to build the island's first street railway.

Construction began that same year, and on November 13, 1876, the first tramcar service opened to the public—making Jamaica one of the earliest adopters of a tramcar system in the Americas. The original service used horse- and mule-drawn cars that ran on iron tracks embedded into Kingston's streets. These early cars were open-sided, wooden vehicles imported from the John

Stephenson Company of New York, a leading manufacturer of the era.

Initial lines radiated out from downtown Kingston (near Parade and King Street) and extended into the growing suburbs. Key routes developed in the late 19th century included:

- Rae Town (East Kingston) – extending toward Kingston Harbour.
- Spanish Town Road (West Kingston) – reaching May Pen Cemetery by 1884.
- Half Way Tree to Constant Spring (North Kingston) – reaching 6 miles north by 1885.
- Inner-city loops, such as the East Queen Street to Paradise Street route by 1879.

By the 1890s, Kingston's tram network had expanded to about 12 miles of track, running dozens of trams with bell-equipped mules alerting pedestrians. Though popular and essential to daily life, the limitations of animal-powered transit—slow speed, limited capacity, and high upkeep—soon became apparent.

In December 1897, a Canadian-backed company, the West India Electric Company (WIEC), purchased the entire horse-drawn tram system with a bold plan to electrify the network. Construction began in June 1898, involving the installation of steel rails, overhead wires, and the building of a central hydroelectric power plant at Bog Walk on the Rio Cobre River.

First Electric Tramcars—1899

On March 31, 1899, Kingston's first electric tramcars began service. The inaugural route symbolically ran from Orange Street, where the new tram depot (or car barn) was located—the operational heart of the electric system—to the foot of King

Street, where the earliest mule-drawn routes had once begun. The transformation was complete by April 1, when the full 25-mile network reopened as a modern electric streetcar system. WIEC imported 30 electric cars—many modeled on those used in Montreal—which ran faster, carried more passengers, and dramatically improved public transit.

In the years that followed, WIEC expanded service to areas like Rockfort, Papine, and Hope Gardens. The trams hauled both passengers and freight, including market carts and banana wagons from outlying districts. In 1923, the Jamaica Public Service Company (JPS) took over both WIEC's electric utility operations and the tramway itself, continuing to manage the growing fleet.

By the mid-1920s, the tram system covered nearly 27 miles of track with around 39 electric tramcars in regular service. It survived natural disasters like the 1907 earthquake, two world wars, and remained Kingston's primary mode of transport for over 70 years.

But by the 1940s, modern buses and private automobiles were on the rise. The tramway—now aging and in need of expensive upgrades—was gradually phased out. On May 10, 1948, the last electric tram made its final journey through Kingston. By 1949, the tramcars had been dismantled and sold for scrap.

Though long gone, Jamaica's tram system left a lasting legacy. It was a pioneering public transit venture that helped shape Kingston's growth and introduced generations to the possibilities of modern transportation in the Caribbean.

1883

The Island's First Telephone System

Just seven years after Alexander Graham Bell patented the telephone in the United States, Jamaica became one of the earliest adopters of the technology in the Caribbean. In 1883, telephone service was officially introduced in Kingston by the West India and Columbia Electric Company, a forerunner to what would later become Cable & Wireless Jamaica—now branded as LIME, short for Landline, Internet, Mobile, Entertainment. The company installed the island's first 50 telephone lines, marking the beginning of a new era in communication.

Initially a private venture, the telephone network began modestly, connecting key locations within the capital. Businesses and government offices were among the first to adopt the new system, recognizing its potential to streamline operations and reduce delays in communication. Early switchboards required manual operation, and only a handful of subscribers could be connected at a time.

Despite its limited reach, the telephone quickly gained importance. By the early 20th century, the network had expanded to other major towns such as Spanish Town and Montego Bay, though true long-distance service across the island remained a future ambition.

The arrival of the telephone in Jamaica was more than a technological novelty—it represented a step toward modernization and greater connectivity. Alongside the development of electricity, trams, and eventually radio, the telephone helped integrate urban centers and paved the way for a more connected society.

1891

The Jamaica International Exhibition & The First Steps Toward Tourism

By the late 19th century, Jamaica remained a British colony struggling to diversify its economy beyond sugar and banana exports. Although its natural beauty, warm climate, and mineral springs had long attracted visitors seeking health benefits, the island had yet to position itself as a true tourist destination. The Jamaica International Exhibition was pivotal in changing how Jamaica was perceived, marking the first major effort to promote its attractions to the world.

Inspired by London's Great Exhibition of 1851, the event was championed by Augustus Constantine Sinclair, head of the Government Printing Office in Jamaica. Initially, Sinclair struggled to gain support for the ambitious project, but momentum built with the arrival of Governor Sir Henry Blake in 1889, who offered critical backing.

Held in Kingston from January 27 to May 2, 1891, the exhibition aimed to showcase Jamaica's natural resources, products, and potential for foreign investment. It attracted exhibits and machinery from Britain, Canada, the United States, and as far away as Russia, exposing Jamaicans to new industries and technologies. While agriculture and commerce were central themes, the exhibition also played a crucial role in positioning Jamaica as a destination for leisure and travel.

Over 300,000 visitors—nearly half of Jamaica's population at the time—attended the event. While the majority were locals, the exhibition also attracted wealthy visitors from Britain and North America. For many, it was their first exposure to the island's scenic beauty, golden beaches, and therapeutic mineral springs as luxury attractions. This exposure helped shift perceptions of Jamaica from a plantation colony to a place of leisure and tropical escape.

Although the exhibition was a financial failure, it planted the seeds for Jamaica's future tourism industry. By the early 20th century, investments in hotels, railways, and marketing campaigns would transform tourism from an idea into a major economic force—one that would eventually rival agriculture as Jamaica's leading industry.

1892
The Arrival of Electricity in Jamaica

Electricity first came to Jamaica in 1892, when the Jamaica Electric Light Company began operations from a coal-burning steam plant on Gold Street in Kingston. The company initially supplied electricity for street lighting and limited commercial use, making Kingston one of the earliest cities in the Caribbean to adopt electric power.

In 1893, the town of Black River in St. Elizabeth became the first in Jamaica to use electricity in a private residence, when the Leyden brothers installed a logwood-fueled generator at their home, Waterloo House. This historic moment marked the beginning of electrification in Jamaica, with Waterloo becoming the first residence on the island to feature electric lighting.

Despite these early breakthroughs, electricity remained limited to urban centers and wealthier communities. It wasn't until the formation of the Jamaica Public Service Company (JPS) in 1923 that a coordinated, island-wide effort was made to expand access to electricity. JPS played a pivotal role in building out the infrastructure necessary for residential and industrial electrification across Jamaica.

In summary, while electricity arrived in Jamaica as early as 1892, its widespread application and integration into daily life unfolded gradually. These early milestones, however, laid the foundation for the island's long-term modernization and industrial growth in the 20th century.

---

c. 1893

The Arrival of Syrians and Lebanese in Jamaica

The exact date of the arrival of the Syrians and Lebanese is not known, but historical records indicate that by the late 19th century, a growing number of families had established themselves on the island.

Fleeing religious persecution and economic hardship under Ottoman rule, most were Christians from Mount Lebanon, then part of Greater Syria—a region that today includes modern Syria and Lebanon. The terms "Syrian" and "Lebanese" are often used interchangeably in early Jamaican records, as national distinctions only emerged after World War I, when France divided the region into separate mandates.

Why Jamaica?

Several factors influenced their decision to settle in Jamaica:

British Protection: As a British colony, Jamaica represented safety and opportunity compared to the instability of Ottoman rule. Britain was widely seen as a land of relative freedom.

Economic Potential: Some immigrants were drawn by Jamaica's push to attract foreign settlers and investment, particularly following the 1891 Jamaica International Exhibition, which promoted the island's agricultural and commercial prospects, attracting international attention and sparking new waves of migration.

Migration Networks: Others arrived via Cuba, Panama, or South America, often moving on after facing poor conditions or limited opportunity.

Early Economic Roles

Upon arrival, many Syrians and Lebanese initially worked in agriculture, especially in the banana trade, which was booming by the 1890s. However, as that sector declined in the early 20th century, most shifted to commerce. Starting as itinerant peddlers, they traveled the island selling dry goods door-to-door —supported by tight-knit ethnic networks that provided credit and business advice.

Over time, they established small retail shops, particularly in dry goods, textiles, and general trade. These family-run businesses became cornerstones of local economies across the island, with many evolving into well-known establishments that lasted for generations.

Cultural Integration

Though they faced racial and social barriers early on, the Syrian and Lebanese communities gradually integrated into Jamaican society, leaving an imprint on its culture:

- Cuisine: Foods such as flatbread (known locally as "Syrian bread"), kibbeh, hummus, and tabbouleh found their way into Jamaican kitchens.
- Language: While Arabic was often spoken in homes, most descendants today speak English and the local dialect, Patois. A few Arabic phrases survive in family circles.
- Intermarriage: Over generations, many families intermarried with other Jamaicans, contributing to the island's multicultural identity.

Notable Contributions

Although small in number compared to other immigrant groups, Syrians and Lebanese left a powerful legacy in Jamaican public life:

- **Politics:** Edward Seaga, one of Jamaica's early Prime Ministers, and Lisa Hanna, a former Miss World and Member of Parliament, are of Lebanese descent.
- **Business:** Prominent families such as the Issas, Matalons, and Ziadies helped build industries ranging from hospitality and retail to construction and manufacturing.

Legacy

By the mid-20th century, Syrians and Lebanese Jamaicans had cemented their place in the island's commercial, political, and cultural life. Their story is one of resilience, entrepreneurship, and adaptation—an example of how even small communities can help shape a nation's identity

---

1899

The Rise of Hydropower and Electrification in Jamaica

The expansion of electricity began at the turn of the 20th century through an ambitious project that reshaped the island's infrastructure and economy. On April 1, 1899, the West India Electric Company (WIEC) completed Jamaica's first major hydroelectric power station on the Rio Cobre River at Bog Walk, St. Catherine. This pioneering facility harnessed river flow to generate electricity, making Jamaica one of the earliest adopters of hydropower in the Caribbean.

Globally, hydropower was still in its infancy. The first hydroelectric plant—the Vulcan Street Plant—opened just 17 years earlier on the Fox River in Appleton, Wisconsin (1882), and the massive Niagara Falls facility followed in 1895. Jamaica's entry into the field in 1899 placed it at the forefront of renewable energy development in the colonial world, well ahead of many countries in the region.

The electricity produced by the Bog Walk plant was used primarily to power Kingston's electric tramcars, marking the dawn of public electric transportation on the island. WIEC had purchased Kingston's horse-drawn tramway system in December 1897 and began electrifying it soon after. By April 1899, electric trams were running along several routes across Kingston, including Harbour Street, King Street, and East Queen Street.

The electric tram system revolutionized urban mobility by replacing horse-drawn carriages with modern transportation powered by hydropower. However, challenges such as inconsistent electricity supply, poorly maintained tracks, and urban flooding occasionally disrupted service. Despite these issues, the trams were a transformative innovation that operated until 1948, when they were phased out in favor of motor buses.

As electricity demand grew across Jamaica, it became clear that scattered power providers were insufficient to meet national needs. In 1923, smaller electricity companies were consolidated into the Jamaica Public Service Company (JPS), which became the island's main electricity distributor. JPS initially focused on urban centers but laid the groundwork for future nationwide electrification.

The foundation laid by the Bog Walk hydroelectric plant and Kingston's electric tram system was more than a technical milestone—it symbolized Jamaica's transition into modernity and highlighted how energy infrastructure could drive social and economic progress on the island.

1903

The First Automobile Arrives in Jamaica

In 1903, the first automobile made its debut on Jamaican soil, signaling the start of a new era in transportation. Imported by the Leyden family of Black River, St. Elizabeth—already known for pioneering technology with early adoption of the telephone and electricity—the vehicle caused quite a stir.

Black River's relatively flat terrain and well-kept roads made it an ideal testing ground. While the car's top speed was modest by today's standards, it represented a leap forward in mobility and innovation. Though still limited to the wealthy elite, the automobile was a symbol of modernity and progress, foreshadowing Jamaica's gradual embrace of mechanized transport.

Over the following decades, automobiles became more common on the island, particularly after road infrastructure improved and import costs decreased. But in 1903, the arrival of that first car was nothing short of revolutionary—a machine that quite literally changed the way Jamaicans moved.

1907

The Kingston Earthquake & Urban Rebuilding

On January 14, 1907, Kingston was devastated by a violent earthquake, one of the deadliest natural disasters in Jamaica's history. In less than a minute, buildings collapsed, streets buckled, and more than 1,000 people were killed. Fires ignited in the wreckage, sweeping through the city and consuming government offices, businesses, and homes. It was this earthquake that caused the partial sinking and tilting of the Royal Artillery House, now known as the Giddy House in Port Royal. This structure, built around 1880, partially sank into the ground due to soil liquefaction during the earthquake, resulting in its characteristic tilt that gives visitors a disorienting sensation when inside.

The destruction was unparalleled—entire neighborhoods were reduced to rubble, and the city's port and commercial district were severely damaged, crippling Jamaica's economy. The colonial government, overwhelmed by the scale of the disaster, relied on British military assistance and international aid to manage the crisis. Makeshift relief camps were set up for the thousands left homeless, while emergency food supplies and medical aid were rushed in to prevent further loss of life.

The disaster, however, forced a transformation. In the aftermath, the government introduced modern building codes, incorporating earthquake-resistant construction techniques to prevent similar devastation in the future. Infrastructure projects followed, leading to improved sanitation, better roads, and a more structured urban layout. Over time, Kingston re-emerged as Jamaica's dominant economic and political center, its reconstruction laying the groundwork for the city's role in the coming push for self-governance.

Additionally, the devastation reinforced the urgent need for urban planning reforms, leading to greater investment in public infrastructure and long-term modernization efforts. Many of the structures built in Kingston's post-earthquake period laid the foundation for its transformation into a financial and administrative hub, solidifying its position as Jamaica's capital in the years leading up to independence and beyond.

1914

The Rise of Marcus Garvey & Jamaica Enters World War I

By 1914, Jamaica was still under British colonial rule, with economic hardship, racial inequality, and political exclusion defining life for the vast majority of Black Jamaicans. While Britain controlled the island's government, local opportunities for education, land ownership, and political participation remained severely limited.

It was in this atmosphere of oppression and growing racial consciousness that Marcus Mosiah Garvey, a young Jamaican journalist and activist, founded the Universal Negro Improvement Association (UNIA). Inspired by his travels in Central America and Britain, where he witnessed the struggles of Black people under colonial rule, Garvey developed a bold vision of Black pride, economic self-sufficiency, and global unity.

The UNIA quickly became a powerful movement, promoting Black empowerment, economic independence, and the idea of African redemption—the belief that people of African descent should unite, reclaim pride in their heritage, and work toward the rebuilding of Africa as a powerful, self-determined continent. His message resonated deeply among Jamaica's working class, and later gained international influence, particularly in the United States. Though Garvey left for the U.S. in 1916, his legacy in Jamaica endured, inspiring future political activism and shaping the emergence of Rastafarianism in the 1930s. Decades later, his contributions to Black empowerment and Jamaican nationalism were formally recognized when he was named one of Jamaica's National Heroes.

Jamaica Enters World War I

While Garvey was launching a movement, the world was on the brink of war. In July 1914, the assassination of Archduke Franz Ferdinand of Austria triggered a chain reaction of alliances, plunging Europe into World War I. As part of the British Empire, Jamaica was automatically drawn into the war when Britain declared war on Germany in August 1914.

Thousands of Jamaicans enlisted in the British West Indies Regiment (BWIR), hoping that their service would earn them greater rights and opportunities. However, they soon found themselves facing harsh conditions, discrimination, and racial segregation within the British military. Many Jamaicans who served on the Western Front, in Egypt, and in the Middle East returned home disillusioned, having fought for an empire that still denied them basic freedoms.

Meanwhile, the war disrupted Jamaica's economy. With global trade routes affected, exports of sugar and bananas suffered, leading to rising unemployment and food shortages. This economic instability heightened social tensions, setting the stage for future labor unrest and anti-colonial resistance.

1920

The Birth of Jamaica's Tourism Industry

By 1920, Jamaica remained a deeply colonial society, with economic power still concentrated in the hands of British elites and foreign corporations. However, a new industry was beginning to take shape—one that would eventually rival agriculture as Jamaica's economic powerhouse.

For decades, Jamaica's economy had been tied to sugar and bananas, but the United Fruit Company, which already controlled much of the banana trade, saw another opportunity—marketing Jamaica as a tropical paradise for wealthy travelers.

Port Antonio, still a major banana shipping hub, began transforming into Jamaica's first luxury destination, largely due to the investments of American entrepreneurs. The Titchfield Hotel, owned by United Fruit Company, became a magnet for millionaires and Hollywood celebrities, who arrived seeking a Caribbean retreat. At the same time, Montego Bay's Doctor's Cave Beach gained international fame for its "healing waters," drawing elite visitors who believed in its therapeutic properties.

While the 1920s marked the emergence of luxury tourism, Jamaica had been a destination for health seekers long before that, due to its renowned mineral springs. Throughout the 19th century, visitors from across the British Empire traveled to Jamaica's Bath Fountain in St. Thomas, Milk River Bath in Clarendon, and later, Rockfort Mineral Bath in Kingston, all famed for their therapeutic waters believed to cure ailments like rheumatism, gout, and skin conditions. These mineral springs were among Jamaica's earliest tourist attractions, laying the foundation for the island's reputation as a wellness retreat.

By 1920, tourism was no longer just about health and healing—it was becoming an economic force. The development of hotels, resorts, and entertainment venues signaled a shift away from Jamaica's dependence on plantation exports toward an economy fueled by leisure, hospitality, and international visitors. Though still reserved for the white and wealthy, the growing tourism sector set the stage for Jamaica's transformation into one of the Caribbean's top travel destinations.

1930

The Rise of Rastafarianism & National Identity

By the early 20th century, Jamaica was a deeply multicultural society, but British colonial rule still dominated political and economic life. Many Jamaicans, particularly the poor and landless, sought a new identity—one rooted in African heritage and spiritual liberation.

The coronation of Haile Selassie I in Ethiopia (1930) was seen by many as the fulfillment of Marcus Garvey's prophecy that a Black king would rise in Africa. This event marked the birth of Rastafarianism, which drew from:

- African spiritual traditions, particularly Kumina and Revivalism
- Christian biblical teachings, especially Old Testament prophecies
- Anti-colonial resistance and Pan-Africanism, with Ethiopia as a symbol of Black empowerment and liberation

At the same time, Jamaican Patois was evolving, blending words from African languages—as well as Hindi, Chinese, Arabic, and English, into the distinct speech pattern we recognize today. This linguistic fusion reflects Jamaica's multicultural history, shaped by waves of immigration and cross-cultural interactions over centuries:

From Hindi (Indian indentured workers, 1845–1917):

- "Chutney" – a popular condiment, now a staple in Jamaican cuisine.
- "Jahaji" – meaning shipmate, used among indentured workers and later absorbed into Patois.
- "Coolie" – originally referring to Indian laborers, though later became a racialized term.

From Chinese (Chinese immigrants, 1854 onward):

- "Pak choy" – from Cantonese, referring to the leafy green vegetable commonly used in Jamaican cooking.
- "Hakka" – originally referring to the Hakka ethnic group, but sometimes used to describe Chinese Jamaicans in general.

From Arabic (Syrian & Lebanese immigrants, 1890s onward):

- "Bushra" – used in business transactions, meaning profit or gain (from Arabic bashar, meaning good news).

Jamaican Patois was more than just a spoken language—it became a symbol of national identity, uniting people from different backgrounds through shared expressions, idioms, and storytelling traditions.

1938

The Labour Riots & the Road to Self-Governance

By 1938, frustration among Jamaica's working class had reached its breaking point. Decades of low wages, exploitative working conditions, and political exclusion had left laborers across the island angry and desperate. The effects of the Great Depression had worsened an already fragile economy, and employers—particularly in the sugar and banana industries—had refused to improve wages despite soaring profits.

The first spark came at the Frome Sugar Estate in Westmoreland, where workers, exhausted by brutal conditions, walked off the job in protest. When the authorities responded with force, the unrest spread rapidly. Soon, Kingston's dockworkers, banana laborers in Portland, and sugar workers in Clarendon joined the movement. Strikes turned into riots, with thousands of Jamaicans taking to the streets, demanding not just fair pay, but fundamental change.

Though sparked by wage disputes, the unrest soon evolved into a broader political awakening, as Jamaicans began demanding not only economic justice but also the right to shape their own future.

Two men emerged as leaders from the crisis.

Alexander Bustamante, a bold and charismatic figure, led workers in Kingston, fearlessly confronting the authorities even after his arrest.

Norman Manley, a highly respected lawyer, worked behind the scenes, pushing for constitutional reforms and negotiations with British authorities.

By the end of 1938, two organizations had been formed that would shape Jamaica's political future:

- The **Bustamante Industrial Trade Union (BITU)**, championing workers' rights.
- The **People's National Party (PNP)**, founded by Manley to fight for self-governance.

For the first time, Jamaica had political movements that directly represented the people, and the path toward independence had begun. From the flames of protest, Jamaica's modern political era was born. These two men would go on to be honored as National Heroes for their role in shaping modern Jamaica.

Part 7

1939 – 1962: The March to Independence

The period from World War II to independence saw Jamaica transition from a British colony to a self-governing nation. The formation of political parties, constitutional changes, and increasing demands for autonomy set the stage for full independence. Economic and social developments, including the growth of the bauxite industry and migration to the UK, reshaped Jamaican society. Finally, on August 6, 1962, Jamaica achieved independence, marking the beginning of a new era as a sovereign nation.

The Birth of Radio Broadcasting

Radio broadcasting in Jamaica officially began on November 17, 1939, with the establishment of the island's first radio station, VP5PZ(*). This pioneering endeavor was led by John Grinan, a local amateur radio operator who broadcast from his home at Seaview Avenue in St. Andrew parish. Grinan had been monitoring international radio transmissions as World War II loomed, and he recognized the potential of radio as a tool for mass communication. He successfully negotiated with the colonial government to adapt his equipment for public service broadcasts, marking the birth of Jamaican radio.

The station's inaugural broadcast featured a statement from Governor Sir Arthur Richards, delivering wartime news and official updates. Initially, VP5PZ operated with a modest schedule, airing half-hour transmissions once a week. Despite its limited reach and resources, the station laid the foundation for modern mass communication in Jamaica.

In 1940, as World War II intensified, the colonial government assumed control of VP5PZ and rebranded it as ZQI(*). This move reflected the government's desire for centralized control over wartime communications. Under its new name, ZQI expanded its operations and launched daily broadcasts on June 3, 1940. Programming grew to include news bulletins and live performances by local artists, overseen by Dennis Gick, a British broadcasting expert and the station's Programme Manager. However, listenership remained limited due to the high cost of radio sets, restricting access primarily to wealthier households or community listening posts.

Despite these challenges, ZQI played a vital role in fostering national unity during wartime by connecting urban and rural audiences through shared news and information. Its early success demonstrated the potential of radio as a medium for mass communication and cultural exchange.

By the late 1940s, however, public criticism regarding the high cost of running ZQI prompted the government to reconsider its role in broadcasting. This led to plans for privatization, setting the stage for the rise of commercial broadcasting in 1950—a turning point that would transform Jamaican media and public life.

(*) –VP5 was the international call sign prefix assigned to British colonies in the Caribbean, including Jamaica. PZ was the individual station identifier. Together, VP5PZ identified the specific amateur (ham) radio station operated by John Grinan in Kingston.
–ZQ was the call sign prefix assigned by the British government for broadcast (non-amateur) stations in overseas territories.
I was the station's specific designation—so ZQI was Jamaica's first official government-operated radio station.
See 1950: The Birth of Commercial Radio

1944

Universal Adult Suffrage & Jamaica's Role in World War II

By 1944, Jamaica stood at a crossroads. The island had long been under British colonial rule, with political power concentrated in the hands of a wealthy elite. However, the labor riots of 1938 had changed everything. The massive uprising—

fueled by years of exploitation, low wages, and poor working conditions—had exposed the deep dissatisfaction of the working class and forced Britain to address the growing demand for political reform.

Universal Adult Suffrage: A Turning Point

After years of pressure from local leaders and trade unions, Universal Adult Suffrage was introduced in 1944, granting every Jamaican over the age of 21—regardless of race, property, or wealth—the right to vote. For the first time, ordinary Jamaicans had the power to shape their government, marking the beginning of a new era in the island's political landscape.

Jamaica's First Elections & the Path to Self-Governance

With voting rights now expanded, Jamaica held its first general elections under this new system. The contest was primarily between two major political parties that had emerged from the labor movement:

- The Jamaica Labour Party (JLP), led by Alexander Bustamante, which championed labor rights and direct political action.
- The People's National Party (PNP), led by Norman Manley, which focused on constitutional reform and self-governance.

The JLP won the elections, and although the British-appointed Governor of Jamaica still held executive power, the formation of an elected House of Representatives was a major step toward self-rule. For centuries, political power had been reserved for the wealthy elite—now, ordinary Jamaicans finally had a voice.

The expansion of suffrage also coincided with changes in Jamaica's economic and social structure:

201

- Chinese Jamaicans strengthened their hold on the retail and grocery trade.
- Indian Jamaicans became more politically active and sought greater economic inclusion.
- Syrian and Lebanese Jamaicans emerged as dominant players in Jamaica's wholesale and textile industries.
- Jewish Jamaicans continued to contribute to the island's legal, commercial, and civic spheres—particularly in urban centers like Kingston.

Suffrage was more than just voting—it was empowerment. It laid the foundation for Jamaica's continued fight for independence and gave the working class the power to shape their future.

Jamaica's Role in World War II

While Jamaica was making political strides at home, it was also playing a crucial role in World War II. In 1944, The Caribbean Regiment was formed, consisting of volunteers from across the British West Indies, including a significant number of Jamaicans. This unit was deployed to North Africa and the Middle East, playing a critical role in British military operations. It was one of the most visible contributions by the Caribbean to the Allied war effort, demonstrating the courage and capability of West Indian soldiers.

Beyond the Caribbean Regiment, Jamaicans served in various branches of the British military:

- **Royal Air Force (RAF):** Over 3,700 Jamaicans served as pilots, mechanics, and ground crew members. Many distinguished themselves in combat and received commendations for bravery.

- **Navy & Merchant Marines:** Jamaican sailors played a critical role in transporting goods and military supplies across the Atlantic, often braving attacks from German U-boats (submarines) that targeted Allied shipping routes.oats.
- **War Support at Home:** Jamaica provided sugar, bauxite, and other key resources critical to the war effort and hosted military bases and training facilities for Allied forces.

Jamaica also played a role in humanitarian efforts. Gibraltar Camp, located on the Mona Estate (now part of the University of the West Indies), housed 1,500 evacuees from Gibraltar and Jewish refugees escaping persecution in Europe. While this was a significant moment in Jamaica's wartime efforts, it was not the first time Jewish people had found refuge on the island. Jews have been part of Jamaica's population since the 16th century, arriving first under Spanish rule as conversos (Jews forced to convert to Christianity) and later openly settling after the British took control in 1655. Over the centuries, Jamaica's Jewish community made notable contributions to commerce, trade, and politics, integrating into the island's diverse society while preserving aspects of their religious and cultural heritage. The presence of Jewish refugees at Gibraltar Camp during World War II was a continuation of this long history of Jewish life in Jamaica, reinforcing the island's identity as a place of multiculturalism, resilience, and refuge.

Despite their sacrifices, many Jamaican soldiers returned home to find that colonial inequalities had not changed. Their wartime experiences, combined with the expansion of political rights, strengthened the demand for full independence.

War's Impact on Jamaica's Economy & the Birth of Tourism

While the war created economic strain, it also led to infrastructure developments that would later transform Jamaica's economy—particularly in tourism. Under the 1940 Destroyers for Bases Agreement with Britain, the United States established several military installations across the island:

- **Vernamfield (Clarendon):** One of the largest U.S. air bases in the Caribbean, used for training, reconnaissance, and aircraft staging. Its location between May Pen and Lionel Town gave it strategic reach along the south coast.
- **Up Park Camp (Kingston):** Portions of the British Army base were used by U.S. forces for logistics, coordination, and administrative functions.
- **Portland Bight (South Coast):** Supported naval patrols and anti-submarine operations critical to defending Allied shipping lanes.
- **Palisadoes Airstrip (Kingston):** Used for military aviation support; this site would later become Norman Manley International Airport, a key hub for post-war civil aviation.

These wartime installations resulted in long-term infrastructure improvements:

- Expansion of airstrips and ports, which later supported commercial air travel and shipping.
- Construction of new roads connecting key towns, laying the foundation for future tourist destinations and internal mobility.

Additionally:

- American soldiers and military officials stationed in Jamaica were among the first to experience the island as a leisure destination.
- Many returned after the war as tourists, helping to spark American interest and contributing to the post-war tourism boom.

As the war ended in 1945, Jamaica began shifting from a purely agricultural economy to one that embraced tourism and industry. In the following decades:

- International travel increased, fueled by commercial aviation.
- Luxury hotels and resorts were developed to cater to wealthy American and British tourists.
- The plantation-based economy gave way to a more diversified economic structure.

1944–A Year of Change

With the war drawing to a close and political power shifting, Jamaica was entering a new era. The introduction of Universal Adult Suffrage gave ordinary Jamaicans a voice in governance for the first time, while their sacrifices in World War II fueled growing demands for national recognition. At the same time, the foundations of a modern economy—tourism, infrastructure, and industrial diversification—were beginning to take shape. Together, these forces laid the groundwork for the nationalist movements and constitutional reforms that would culminate in full independence by 1962.

1945

The End of World War II & Jamaica's Post-War Transformation

As World War II came to an end in 1945, Jamaica stood at a crossroads. Thousands of Jamaicans had served in the British armed forces, with many fighting in the Royal Air Force (RAF) or the Caribbean Regiment. Their service had fueled expectations that returning soldiers would be met with greater rights, opportunities, and social reforms. However, upon their return, they found that Jamaica remained a colony, still under British rule, and still struggling with economic and social inequality.

Impact of the War on Jamaica

The war had drawn many Jamaicans into global affairs like never before. Over 3,700 Jamaicans joined the RAF, working as pilots, ground crew, and mechanics. Others served in the Caribbean Regiment, which was deployed in the Middle East and North Africa. At home, the island played a role in the Allied war effort by hosting military bases and serving as a strategic outpost for British and American forces.

The Gibraltar Camp, established on the former Mona Estate, housed 1,500 evacuees from Gibraltar and provided refuge to Jewish migrants fleeing persecution in Europe. This camp became a symbol of Jamaica's wartime involvement beyond just supplying troops.

Yet, despite these contributions, Jamaicans did not return to a transformed society. The same colonial structures remained in place, leading to frustration among ex-servicemen who had fought for democratic ideals abroad but saw little change at home. Many of them became politically active, joining trade unions and political movements that sought greater self-government and social reforms.

Economic Shifts and Infrastructure Development

The war also affected Jamaica's economy. The demand for Jamaican sugar and bananas had increased during the war, temporarily boosting exports. However, after the war, global markets shifted, and Jamaica faced economic uncertainty. Additionally, the infrastructure built during the war, particularly improved airstrips, roads, and ports, would later support Jamaica's emerging tourism industry.

American soldiers and officials stationed in Jamaica had experienced the island's beaches, climate, and entertainment, generating interest in Jamaica as a travel destination. By the late 1940s, this would contribute to the early growth of the tourism industry, shifting Jamaica's economy away from a strict dependence on agriculture.

The Push for Political Change

The war had set the stage for greater political engagement. In 1944, Universal Adult Suffrage was introduced, giving all Jamaicans over the age of 21 the right to vote for the first time. This historic change meant that Jamaica was moving toward greater self-rule, but full independence was still nearly two decades away.

The returning war veterans, along with labor activists and political leaders like Alexander Bustamante and Norman

Manley, played a critical role in demanding further political reforms. Their efforts laid the groundwork for the push toward self-government and, ultimately, independence in 1962.

Though World War II had ended, the struggle for equality and self-determination in Jamaica was far from over. The post-war years would become a defining period of political awakening and reform, as Jamaicans pushed forward on the long road to independence.

1950

The Birth of Commercial Radio

The voice of a nation is shaped by its ability to communicate—and through that expression, identity is born.
— Author

The establishment of VP5PZ in 1939 and its evolution into ZQI by 1940 marked the beginning of radio broadcasting in Jamaica. Over the next decade, ZQI became a vital platform for wartime news, live performances, and public service programming, connecting urban and rural communities despite challenges such as limited access to radio sets. As the station grew, it showcased the potential of radio as a unifying force and a medium for cultural exchange. However, by the late 1940s, mounting operational costs and public criticism prompted the colonial government to seek alternative solutions for sustaining broadcasting services.

The year 1950 was transformative. Facing financial constraints and mounting public criticism over ZQI's operational costs, the colonial government issued a broadcasting license to the Jamaica Broadcasting Company (JBC)—a subsidiary of the British Rediffusion Group. On May 1, 1950, JBC took over ZQI's operations and rebranded it as Radio Jamaica and Rediffusion Network (RJR).

First Commercial Broadcast

RJR aired its first broadcast on July 9, 1950, officially launching commercial radio under its new call sign. This transition introduced advertisements and sponsored programming as primary sources of income—a significant shift from government-funded operations. While this model initially faced resistance—listener complaints about interruptions from advertisements—it proved sustainable over time.

To ensure accessibility across rural areas where personal radios were scarce, RJR distributed wireless receiving sets to approximately 200 designated listening posts such as schools, police stations, and village stores. This innovative rediffusion service allowed communities without personal radios to tune into daily broadcasts.

By 1951, RJR had transitioned into a full-fledged commercial broadcaster with daily programming that included music, educational content, live events, and cultural discussions. The station quickly became an integral part of Jamaican life, bridging gaps between Kingston and rural parishes while promoting a sense of shared identity during colonial rule. The station also showcased local talent through live performances and cultural programming, solidifying its role as a platform for Jamaican voices.

Breaking Barriers

RJR revolutionized news dissemination in Jamaica by breaking the dominance of printed media. For many Jamaicans— especially those who were illiterate or lacked funds to buy newspapers—radio became the quickest and most accessible way to stay informed about current events. During elections and other pivotal moments leading up to independence, RJR provided real-time analysis and results, fostering political engagement across all social classes.

Hurricane Charlie Coverage

One defining moment for RJR was its coverage of Hurricane Charlie on August 17, 1951, which struck Jamaica directly for the first time in decades. Despite widespread devastation that resulted in over 150 deaths and left thousands homeless, RJR crews worked tirelessly during the storm itself to maintain broadcasts. Most transmitters and wired Rediffusion lines were knocked out—with only one subscriber still able to receive service—but the station's determination ensured that critical updates reached as many listeners as possible during Jamaica's deadliest natural disaster of the 20th century.

Cultural Impact

RJR also played a pivotal role in democratizing access to music at a time when record players were prohibitively expensive for most Jamaicans. It introduced audiences to new genres, international and local music, ranging from classical music to mento—the first popular Jamaican music form—and later ska as Jamaica's recording industry grew.

Technological advancements further solidified RJR's influence. In 1953, it became the first station in the British Commonwealth to broadcast regularly scheduled programs on FM using transmitters installed at Coleyville, Manchester, and Tinson Pen, Kingston.

Conclusion

RJR's mandate to cover the entire island transformed it into Jamaica's primary source of communication through music programming, regular newscasts, dramas, discussions, concerts, and other forms of entertainment. It not only challenged newspapers' dominance but also united Jamaicans across urban and rural divides during a transformative era in the nation's history. As Jamaica moved toward independence, RJR stood at the forefront of information dissemination—reliable during crises like Hurricane Charlie while also shaping cultural identity through its diverse programming.

For when a nation can speak and share its ideas openly and widely, it develops a unique cultural voice—and through that, identity is born.
—Author

—See 1939-40 for Jamaica's early years of Radio.

<hr />

1952

The Rise of Jamaica's Bauxite Industry

By the early 1950s, Jamaica was on the brink of an economic transformation. While sugar and bananas had long dominated the island's exports, a new industry was emerging—one that would propel Jamaica onto the world stage as a major player in global mining and industrial production.

The key to this transformation was bauxite, the raw material used to produce aluminum. Although deposits had been discovered in the 1940s, it wasn't until 1952 that the first large-scale commercial shipments of Jamaican bauxite were made, marking the beginning of what would soon become one of the island's largest industries.

Jamaica Becomes a Global Bauxite Powerhouse

- In 1952, the first major shipment of bauxite left Jamaica, signaling the country's entry into the global aluminum market.
- Foreign corporations, including Alcan, Reynolds, and Kaiser, quickly moved in, establishing large-scale mining operations.
- By the late 1950s, Jamaica had become the world's second-largest producer of bauxite, trailing only Australia.

The boom brought jobs, infrastructure improvements, and new economic opportunities, but it also came with challenges. The bauxite industry was controlled by foreign companies, meaning much of the wealth flowed out of Jamaica rather than staying within local communities. Additionally, mining operations led to environmental degradation, raising concerns about land loss and sustainability.

While the bauxite boom brought economic expansion and jobs, it also exposed deep structural issues. The industry was dominated by U.S. and Canadian corporations, meaning most profits flowed overseas rather than into local communities. Environmental degradation, land disputes, and the limited reinvestment of earnings sparked growing nationalist calls for greater Jamaican control. As global aluminum prices fluctuated, the island's increasing dependence on bauxite created new economic vulnerabilities—pressures that would fuel the push for nationalization in the 1970s.

1953

Full Ministerial Government: A Nation Takes Control of Its Future

In 1953, Jamaica took a significant step toward self-governance with the introduction of Full Ministerial Government. This reform came through constitutional amendments that established the position of Chief Minister and allowed elected Jamaican ministers to oversee specific portfolios such as education, agriculture, and finance. This reform marked a departure from direct colonial administration and empowered local leaders to take charge of domestic governance.

Alexander Bustamante, leader of the Jamaica Labour Party (JLP), became Jamaica's first Chief Minister in 1953. His administration prioritized pragmatic governance, including land reform and economic development. While his tenure ended in 1955 following an electoral defeat, Bustamante's leadership symbolized the growing influence of Jamaican political leaders in shaping the country's future.

1955 — Norman Manley Wins Election

In 1955, Norman Manley and the People's National Party (PNP) won the general election, and Manley succeeded Bustamante as Chief Minister. Under Manley's leadership, Jamaica advanced further toward autonomy.

1957 — Constitutional Changes Introduce the Role of Premier

By 1957, the Executive Council evolved into a Cabinet led by a Premier, consolidating political authority and reducing the powers of the British Governor. Although defense, foreign affairs, and security remained under British control, the Governor was now required to consult the Jamaican Cabinet on internal matters.

The move toward ministerial governance was driven by both global and local forces. Internationally, the post–World War II era saw a wave of decolonization as former colonies sought autonomy. Locally, leaders like Norman Manley—who had championed universal suffrage in 1944—pushed for constitutional reform and internal self-rule. Together, these developments set Jamaica firmly on a path toward independence. Though Jamaica remained officially a Crown Colony, the introduction of ministerial government signaled that the colonial era was drawing to a close.

For the first time, Jamaicans saw leaders from their own communities occupying the highest offices of local power. Political parties were no longer symbolic—they had real influence. The dream of independence was no longer distant—it was now inevitable.

The question was no longer *if* Jamaica would become an independent nation—but *when*.

Key Changes in 1953:

- Jamaica's first locally led government was established through Full Ministerial Government.
- Alexander Bustamante became Jamaica's first Chief Minister, heading the new Cabinet.

- Jamaican ministers gained control over domestic portfolios like education, agriculture, and finance.
- The British Governor retained authority over defense, foreign policy, and national security but was now required to consult the Jamaican Cabinet on local matters.

These reforms laid the groundwork for subsequent milestones such as Jamaica's involvement in the West Indies Federation (1958), its withdrawal following a 1961 referendum, and ultimately independence in 1962.

1958

The West Indies Federation: A Short-Lived Union

As Jamaica moved closer to self-governance, Britain sought a different path for its Caribbean colonies—one that would unite them under a single federal state. The solution was the West Indies Federation, established in 1958, which brought together ten British Caribbean territories, including Jamaica, Trinidad and Tobago, and Barbados. The goal was to create a political and economic union that would transition into full independence from Britain as a single nation, similar to how Canada and Australia had become independent federations.

For Britain, this approach was practical—managing multiple small colonies was expensive, and federation would allow for a more efficient transition to self-rule. However, from the outset, the federation faced major obstacles:

- Geographical Challenges – The territories were scattered across the Caribbean, making communication and transportation difficult.
- Economic Disparities – Some islands had stronger economies than others, leading to concerns about financial burden-sharing.
- Political Tensions – Many Caribbean leaders had differing visions of how the federation should function.

For Jamaica, the biggest issue was economic. As the largest and wealthiest member, Jamaica was expected to shoulder much of the financial responsibility. Many Jamaicans, including prominent politicians like Alexander Bustamante, questioned whether the island would benefit from federation or if it would be better off pursuing independent nationhood.

While the federation initially raised hopes of Caribbean unity, it soon became clear that internal divisions would threaten its survival. The fate of the federation rested on whether Jamaicans truly wanted to be part of it—a question that would be answered in a national referendum just a few years later.

<hr />

1961

Jamaica Votes to Leave the Federation

By 1961, support for the West Indies Federation in Jamaica had weakened significantly. Many Jamaicans believed the island would be held back by the economic struggles of the smaller islands, while others felt that federation offered little benefit compared to full independence. The decision on Jamaica's future in the federation was put to the people in a historic referendum—the first of its kind in Jamaica.

On September 19, 1961, Jamaicans went to the polls to decide whether to remain in the West Indies Federation or to pursue full independence. The results were clear:

- YES (Stay in the Federation): 216,371 votes (39.2%)
- NO (Leave the Federation): 251,776 votes (60.8%)

With nearly 61% voting to leave, the decision sealed Jamaica's path toward full independence. Following the referendum, Alexander Bustamante—who had campaigned against federation—announced that Jamaica would begin negotiations for independence from Britain.

Jamaica's withdrawal from the West Indies Federation was the beginning of the end for the union. With its largest and most powerful member gone, the federation collapsed in 1962, and the other islands pursued their own paths to independence.

For Jamaica, the referendum was a defining moment—it marked the final step in breaking away from colonial rule and embracing nationhood on its own terms.

1962

An Independent Nation is Born

On August 6, 1962, after more than 300 years of British colonial rule, Jamaica officially became an independent nation. The Union Jack was lowered, and in its place, the black, green, and gold flag of Jamaica was hoisted for the first time, symbolizing the country's resilience, natural beauty, and hope for the future.

Though Jamaica was now independent, it remained a constitutional monarchy within the Commonwealth, with Queen Elizabeth II as the ceremonial Head of State. Her role was represented on the island by a Governor-General, ensuring continuity of diplomatic ties without interfering in Jamaica's governance.

The streets of Kingston erupted in celebration—thousands gathered at National Stadium, while church bells rang and fireworks illuminated the night sky. Across the island, parishes held processions, music and dancing filled the streets, and communities came together to mark the birth of a new era.

Sir Alexander Bustamante was sworn in as Jamaica's first Prime Minister, leading a newly formed government that now had full control over domestic policies and internal affairs. However, while independence was a moment of national pride, it also came with immense challenges.

The Road to Independence

Jamaica's journey to self-rule had been long and complex. The push for political autonomy had gained momentum in the 1930s with the labor riots, which exposed economic disparities and social injustices under British rule. By the 1940s, Universal Adult Suffrage had given Jamaicans the right to vote, and in the 1950s, constitutional reforms expanded local governance.

Jamaica briefly participated in the West Indies Federation (1958–1962)—a British attempt to unify Caribbean colonies into a single political entity. However, Jamaicans rejected the Federation in a 1961 referendum, preferring full independence rather than shared governance with smaller Caribbean islands.

This decision set the stage for the final negotiations with Britain, culminating in independence the following year.

Challenges of Nationhood

Independence brought both promise and uncertainty. While Jamaicans now had political autonomy, the country still faced significant economic and structural hurdles:

- **Economic Dependence:** Major industries, including bauxite, sugar, and banking, were still largely controlled by foreign corporations, leaving Jamaica vulnerable to external economic pressures.
- **Land and Wealth Inequality:** A large percentage of arable land remained in the hands of a small, wealthy elite, while many Jamaicans struggled to access land for farming or housing.
- **Industrial Development:** The economy was heavily reliant on agriculture and raw material exports, and there was an urgent need to develop manufacturing, infrastructure, and education to sustain growth.
- **Social Cohesion:** While independence united the nation, political divisions were already emerging between the two dominant parties—the Jamaica Labour Party (JLP) and the People's National Party (PNP)—which would soon shape the country's political landscape.

A Multicultural Nation Moving Forward

Despite the challenges, Jamaica's independence was a milestone in the global movement against colonialism, inspiring other Caribbean nations to follow suit. The island's multicultural fabric, shaped by centuries of migration—including Africans, Indians, Chinese, Syrians, Lebanese, Jews and Europeans— became one of its greatest strengths. Unlike many societies where ethnic groups remained separate, Jamaicans—regardless of background—blended into a vibrant national identity, united by music, language, and a shared vision for the future.

It was not the end of the journey, but the beginning of a new struggle—one for economic self-sufficiency, social justice, and political stability. The road ahead would not be easy, but for the first time in history, the future of Jamaica was in Jamaican hands.

Epilogue

Jamaica: Forged by Fire, Carried by Flame

Jamaica was born of fire.

From deep beneath an ancient sea, tectonic plates clashed, a slow dance atop a sea of fire. The occasional stumble, unleashing violent quakes that crack the crust, sending molten rock rushing toward its fiery master—the Sun. To the east, the battle raged hotter still, lifting the land skyward and birthing the Blue Mountains in a plume of fire and ash. From these convulsions of earth and flame, an island emerged—raw, wild, and magnificent.

Time softened what fire had shaped. Rain carved valleys, clothing hills with verdant forests as birds sang, and rivers danced their way to the sea. It was a land waiting for a people.

They came in canoes, riding ocean currents and chasing ancestral legends. The Arawaks became Taíno—"the good people"—and with them, Jamaica's human story began.

Then came conquest. Slavery. Rebellion. Resistance. Through centuries of foreign rule and bondage, the fires never truly died. They merely shifted—from the belly of the earth to the hearts of its people. Smoldering in silence—then flaring into revolt.

The drums of Tacky's Rebellion, the spark of Sam Sharpe, the silent courage of Nanny. The Maroons fought from the mountains. The enslaved fought from the fields. And the free

221

built villages with faith as their mortar. From Morant Bay to Montego Bay, heroes rose, the island pushed forward, step by halting step.

In 1962, the last chain was broken. The Union Jack lowered. The black, green, and gold rose, a phoenix rising, seeking its true potential. Jamaica stood tall—not because the fire had vanished, but because it had been harnessed. Refined. Reborn.

Since then, the island has given more than its share to the world. Athletes who outrun history. Artists whose soundtrack is its journey. Scholars, soldiers, scientists, poets. Its culture pulses across continents. Its people, fierce in pride, warm in spirit. No longer a colony. Forever a nation.

And still the mountains stand, the rivers run, and the fire burns bright.

The fires that forged this land still live—no longer beneath the surface, but in the soul of a nation unshackled, a people unbroken, and history unfinished.

Jamaica's journey continues.

Beyond the Book

This book represents a curated and expanded edition of the core historical timeline originally developed as part of a larger body of work at jamaicatimeline.com, a website created under the Fiwi Roots Project (fiwiroots.com/about.html).

The website offers an even broader view of Jamaica's development—featuring dedicated sections on the island's people, music, industry, and cultural identity, along with visual aids, maps, and educational tools.

New material is added regularly, including extended essays, historical profiles, and multimedia content that builds on topics introduced in this book.

Whether you're a researcher, teacher, student, or simply a curious reader, the site is designed as an open and growing resource for deeper exploration.

This website is one of several created as part of the Fiwi Roots Project —a nonprofit initiative dedicated to preserving Jamaica's heritage, history, and culture. The project also sponsors the Young Dreamers Scholarship, which supports students from under-resourced rural communities across the island.

To learn more, visit:

🔗 jamaicatimeline.com

🔗 fiwiroots.com/about.html

Join the ongoing journey through Jamaica's past—and its future.

www.ingramcontent.com/pod-product-compliance
Lightning Source LLC
Chambersburg PA
CBHW071421090426
42737CB00011B/1532